I Ching Prescriptions
Choosing Change

By Adele Aldridge, Ph.D.

© Adele Aldridge 2011
All Rights Reserved

ISBN: 1-884178-25-1
EAN-13: 978-1-884178-25-2

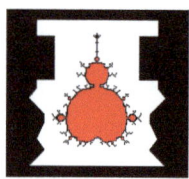

Kairos Center
PO Box 142086
Austin, Texas 78714

Also by Adele Aldridge
I Ching Record Book: Tools for Crating a Synchronicity Journal
www.ichingshop.com
www.ichingmeditations.com

The 64 Hexagrams in Circular Arrangement

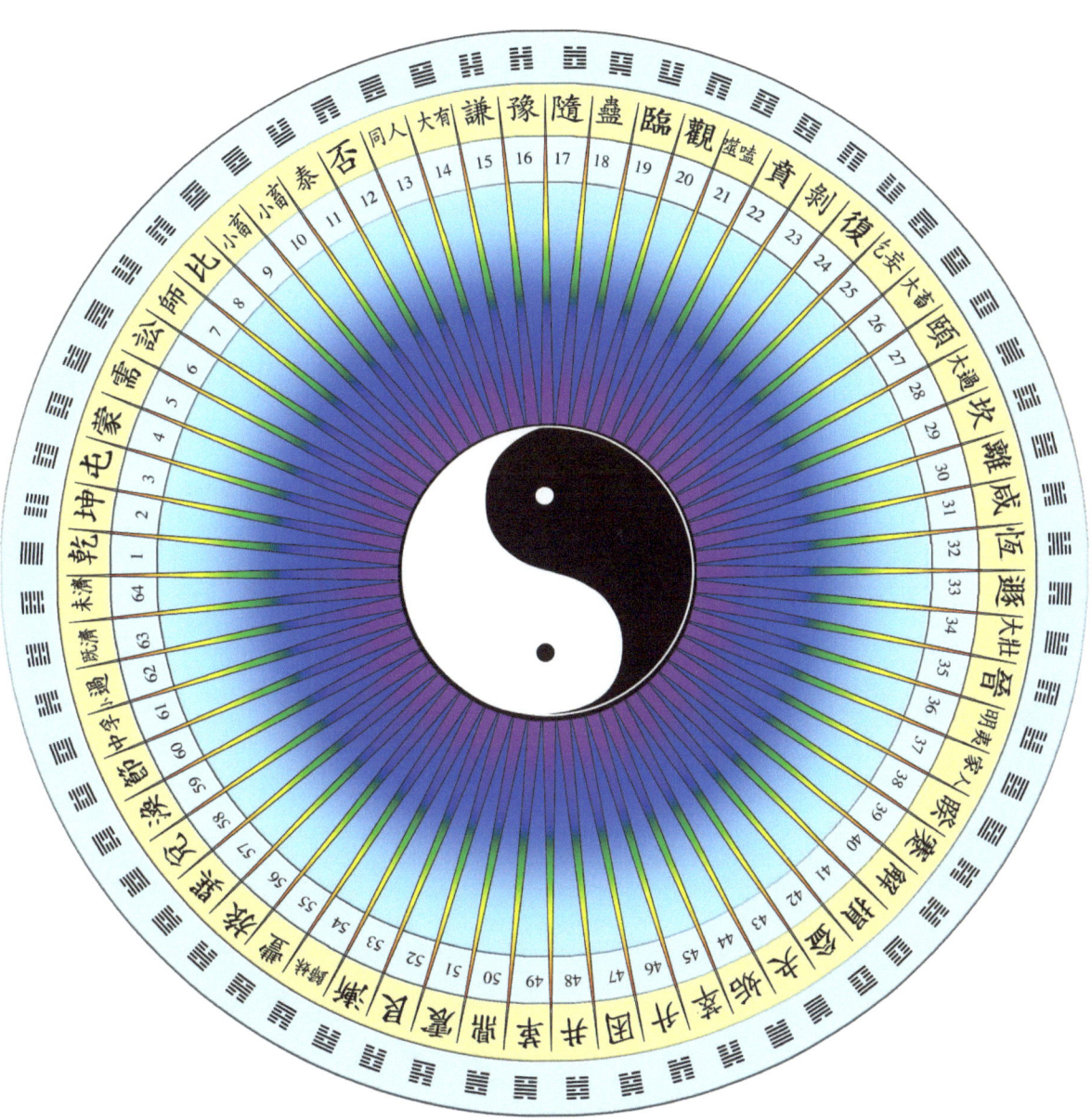

Contents

Foreword	6
Introduction	7
The Trigrams and Their Various Associations	9
Trigram Images	10
What are I Ching Prescriptions?	12
I Ching Prescriptions	16
I Ching Chart for When All Lines Change	18
Trigram Language	20
Health Questions	22
Trigrams Associated with the Body for Health Questions	23
I Ching and Chakra Meditation	24
The Chakras	25
How to Toss Coins to Receive Your I Ching Hexagram	26
Hexagram Key Chart	27
01. Creativity	28
02. Receptivity	29
03. Sprouting/Giving Birth	30
04. Youthful Folly	31
05. Waiting	32
06. Conflict	33
07. The Army/Discipline	34
08. Union	35
09. Small Accumulating	36
10. Treading/Conduct	37
11. Peace	38
12. Standstill/Stop!	39
13. Friends in Community	40
14. Wealth	41
15. Modesty	42
16. Enthusiasm	43
17. Following	44
18. Corruption/Therapy	45
19. Approach	46
20. Contemplation/Viewing	47
21. Biting Through	48
22. Grace/Adornment	49
23. Splitting Apart	50
24. Return/The Turning Point	51
25. Innocence	52
26. Accumulating Great Power	53
27. Providing Nourishment	54
28. Over Loaded/Crisis	55

29. The Abysmal Water	56
30. The Clinging Fire	57
31. Influence/Courtship	58
32. Duration/Marriage	59
33. Retreat	60
34. Great Power	61
35. Progress/Flourishing	62
36. Darkening of the Light	63
37. The Family/The Clan	64
38. Opposition	65
39. Obstruction/Limping	66
40. Deliverance/Release	67
41. Decrease	68
42. Increase	69
43. Break-through	70
44. Coming to Meet/Coupling	71
45. Gathering Together	72
46. Pushing Upward	73
47. Exhaustion/Oppression	74
48. The Well	75
49. Revolution/Molting	76
50. The Caldron/Transformation	77
51. Shock	78
52. Keeping Still/Meditation	79
53. Gradual Progress	80
54. The Second Wife	81
55. Abundance	82
56. The Wanderer	83
57. Gentle Penetration	84
58. Joy	85
59. Dispersion	86
60. Limitation	87
61. Inner Truth	88
62. Many Small Things	89
63. After Completion	90
64. Before Completion	91
Hexagram 10 — Treading	92
Earlier Heaven: Primal Arangment of Trigrams	96
Later Heaven: Inner World Arangment of Trigrams	97
Bibliography	98
Afterword	99

Foreword

Adele Aldridge has devoted much of her lifetime to exploring the beauties and mysteries of the I Ching. Her art is gorgeous and her thoughtful I Ching comments spring from a long familiarity with the topic.

It pleases me to see that her *I Ching Prescriptions* book asks you to familiarize yourself with the dynamic of the whole hexagram, including an overview of each of the six lines in the hexagram. This is the only way to get the full import of the hexagram's energy. This gives you a chance to realize the various likely courses your result may take, depending on your approach to the situation.

To test out her *Prescriptions* approach, I tried it myself via a sample - i.e., I looked up a *Prescription* for an issue that I have now.

My issue was this: lately I have been so busy that it has tired me out considerably. After going to lecture on an IONS Consciousness cruise, I came back surprised to discover how refreshed I am now by the trip. Things seem to go easier and I have more vitality.

I first asked the I Ching synchronicity to comment on this situation I have been feeling and then I opened the *I Ching Prescriptions* book at random. Here is the answer I got: Prescription for hexagram 40: *Deliverance/Release.*

It feels good when any kind of tension has been released. Clear up lingering issues so that you begin with a fresh start. Do not dwell on transgressions made against you. Pardon and forgive. Get on with the new. Solve problems that have held you back in struggle and you will have more energy. You may wake up from something that you have been in denial about. Be like the rain pouring down washing things away as the seeds of the new begin to germinate.

It seems to me that this answer is quite correct and appropriate for my situation.

I recommend this book *I Ching Prescriptions* for its beauty, wisdom, and practical advice. It shows how the I Ching oracle invites and even coaxes the user into developing these qualities. They exist abundantly in this book.

Katya Walter, Ph.D.

Introduction

Who Needs I Ching Prescriptions?

- I Ching Geeks — those of you who already are consulting the I Ching, are familiar with more than one interpretation and enjoy reading other perspectives on the subject.
- The person who is somewhat interested, is not a skeptic, likes to have an I Ching reading done for them but so far has not been motivated to delve more deeply into I Ching philosophy.
- The person who is a skeptic concerning the I Ching and has turned it down as a possibility to take seriously.
- The person who has no idea of what the I Ching is and could benefit by its wisdom.

I will address this last group first.

What is the I Ching?

As of this writing there are close to 2,000 books related to the I Ching listed on Amazon. The subject is vast and complex. This book has a somewhat different perspective on how to use the wisdom of the I Ching, so for the benefit of readers who need some background on the I Ching to help understand what the *I Ching Prescriptions* are I will give a brief overview here of the subject. If you want to learn more about the I Ching then you will enjoy investigating the history of the I Ching and/or other perspectives on the subject.

I Ching means, "Book of Changes." *The Book of Changes* has only one law that remains constant: The only thing that never changes is change itself.

I Ching is a philosophy, not a religion, although there are many who consult it religiously. This philosophy dates back to the origins of Chinese civilization, evolving over centuries of time as Chinese writing and culture developed. This philosophy is based on the premise that everything in the universe arises out of two forces, Yang and Yin, the Chinese words for masculine and feminine energy.

I Ching philosophy says that if you follow the way of nature you will find the right way and right time for action in your own life. I Ching can be viewed as a part of nature herself as the human psyche reflects back, as a collective, where it stands within the whole. By consulting the I Ching we can recognize ourselves as part of nature and that the universe and we are one organism.

I Ching is the Original Computer

Because the archetypes in the I Ching were programmed over centuries by the input of many human psyches the evolution of I Ching philosophy, *The Book of Changes,* is a collective response to the human condition and part of the collective unconscious. The I Ching might be experienced as a psychic computer, revealing itself to us through thousands of years of time.

The traditional way of consulting I Ching is as a tool for divination which requires interactivity based on the concept of synchronicity, a term coined by Carl

Jung. The power of the I Ching is only activated through the interaction of the human mind.

The Book of Changes is not meant to be read from cover to cover in linear fashion the way Western texts are written. While the I Ching is used for divination, it is not meant to be a fortune-telling device, but guidance for the best possible behavior in a given situation. One brings a question to seek counsel from the book much the way one might seek help from a therapist, priest or any such wisdom figure.

While the *Book of Changes* incorporates an inter-play of symbols derived from the elements of nature it contains layers of symbols, one within the other where symbols are used to describe other symbols. Because the nature of a symbol always points to something beyond itself, the meaning can never be pinned down but is always open to each new reader. It is no wonder then that many people find this book of wisdom obscure.

I Ching symbols

The I Ching is comprised of 64 situations, all derived from the combination of 2 lines, yang (whole) ———— and yin (opened) —— —— .

There are 4 combinations of the 2 lines.

When the yin and yang lines are combined in sets of 3 they form the 8 trigrams (See chart below.) Each trigram is named for a force in nature and has other attributes associated with it. (See chart on page 9.) When the trigrams are combined in sets of 2 each they form the 64 possible combinations that form the hexagrams.

The 8 images of nature that the I Ching is based on are: Heaven, Thunder, Water, Mountain, Earth, Wind/Wood, Fire and Lake. The images illustrating each of the trigrams on pages 10 and 11 are from my work on interpreting the I Ching called, *I Ching Meditations,* a work in process. I include them here to give a face to the 8 symbols of nature depicted for notation in the I Ching.

The origins of the I Ching pre-date literacy. We can not begin to imagine today what it was like to live in an environment that did not include the Internet, telephone, electricity — you name it — and be solely dependant upon nature. The people of prehistorical China had to have respect for and awe of nature that in many ways has been lost to our consciousness today. The ancient Chinese did not see themselves as separate from the environment in which they lived.

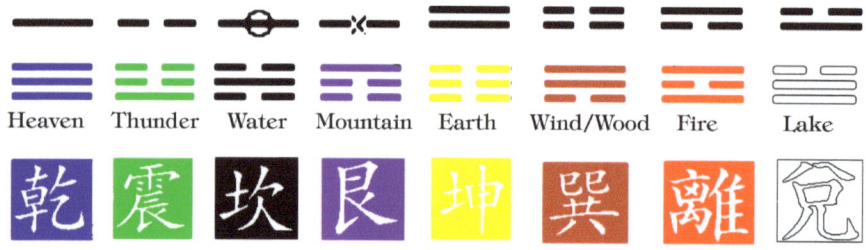

The Trigrams and Their Various Associations

Trigrams	Attribute	Animal	Body	Family	Direction	Color
☰ Ch'ien • Creative Heaven	Creativity Strength	Dragon & Horse	Head	Father	Northwest	Indigo
☳ Kên * Arousing Thunder	Action	Dragon	Feet	Eldest Son	East	Green
☵ K'an • Abysmal Water	Danger	Pig	Ear	Second Son	North	Black
☶ Chên • Keeping Still Mountain	Stillness	Dog	Hand	Youngest Son	Northeast	Purple
☷ K'un • Receptive Earth	Receptivity	Mare & Cow	Belly	Mother	Southwest	Yellow
☴ Sun • Gentle Wind & Wood	Penetration	Fowl	Thighs	Eldest Daughter	Southeast	Scarlet
☲ Li • Clinging Fire	Brightness Dependence	Pheasant	Eye	Second Daughter	South	Crimson
☱ Tui • Joyous Lake	Joy Pleasure	Sheep	Mouth	Youngest Daughter	West	White

About Colors Used for These Lines of Trigrams

I arrived at the colors associated with each trigram from the book, *I Ching, The Classic Chinese Oracle of Change* translated by Rudolf Ritsema and Stephen Karcher, published by Barnes & Noble in 1995. However when I did research for this book I noticed that some other I Ching authors didn't associate the same colors with some of the trigrams. I found black, yellow and blood red attributed to The Receptive Earth; Thunder was both green and yellow; Wind/Wood were both scarlet and white, and Abysmal Water both black and blood red. For the sake of time and effort I will continue to use the colors from my original source.

As I have been putting this book together the effect of seeing the trigrams in color has caused me to view the hexagrams more as what they are — two trigrams interacting with each other. I'm used to seeing these six lines in black on white, defining the lines as one statement. Whereas when I view the hexagrams with both colors, I get an additional hint of meaning, reminding me of the meaning of the trigrams contained within each hexagram.

Trigram Images 1 — 4

The Creative Heaven

The Arousing Thunder

The Abysmal Water

The Keeping Still Mountain

Trigram Images 5 — 8

The Receptive Earth

The Gentle Wind & Wood

The Clinging Fire

The Joyous Lake

What are I Ching Prescriptions?

The *I Ching Prescriptions* are a different way of working with the I Ching. Many people wonder how could anyone take seriously an answer to a question arrived at by tossing coins. For this reason they decide that the I Ching is not for them. You don't have to believe in synchronicity. You don't have to take the time to understand the poetic symbolic language of the I Ching. When people dismiss the I Ching because it relies on random chance they miss out on the philosophy imbedded within it. A philosophy, based on nature that has survived for thousands of years has a message worth pondering.

I wrote this book for people who are not drawn to the more complex translations that often require one to read the responses like one would a dream. Not everyone responds to symbolic language. I wanted to make the Prescriptions direct and easy to use, just like taking a pill might be. I don't know how an aspirin works. I just know that it does. This does not mean I do not appreciate all the other I Ching interpretations. I get benefit from them. I love symbols, poetry and symbolic language. If I didn't I would not have been consulting the I Ching for so many years.

How the *I Ching Prescriptions* are Formulated

These *I Ching prescriptions* are not intended to be a replacement for any of the many I Ching interpretations in publication. Forty years ago there was very little I Ching interpretation available. It was Carl Jung's forward in Richard Wilhelm's translation that first hooked me into the I Ching and remains my favorite version. However I frequently read several different interpretations of I Ching and benefit from various other perspectives. Because consulting the philosophy of I Ching is a subjective experience for the individual asking the question, I find all interpretations interesting.

While I have been studying and consulting the I Ching for over forty years, I cannot read Chinese so I rely on and am inspired by other translations and interpretations. They are all slightly different, depending on the subjective viewpoint of the writer. I pondered and absorbed meaning from these texts by distilling into a condensed essence a small script that has meaning for each of the 64 situations that the hexagrams describe.

If you are new to the I Ching, you might begin with one interpretation that you find relevant and then go on to read others. In the Bibliography you will find a list of interpretations of the I Ching that helped me to synthesize the material for these Prescriptions.

How is the Prescription Method Different?

I have been involved with the I Ching for so long because it works. Synchronicity happens. So why have I created a different method in tandem with my practice of throwing the coins and relying on "chance" for my I ching answers?

First I need to give some background as to how I arrived at creating the prescriptions. If one is using the I Ching as a tool for divination one consults the I Ching by asking a question and then relies on the synchronicity of casting the coins or yarrow sticks. Because the Chinese language is not linear but pictorial I felt that giving the work images to ponder, along with linear text, was a broader experience for the meaning of the text however subjective that may be.

Back in the dark ages before the Internet and development of the personal computer, I began my saga of interpreting the I Ching with a set of black and white woodcuts integrating the use of astrology symbols with the images for the trigrams. I made 64 prints, one for each hexagram. I laminated them onto canvasses and strung together to hang in a large wall construction. I also made two sets of these prints on rice paper and hand bound them into books, 16" X 20" in size and after that I made a similar set in color. Next I translated these designs into large acrylic paintings 36" X 48." I exhibited these works in an exhibition in the Greenwich library, Greenwich, Connecticut in 1972.

The next generation of creating images inspired by I Ching is a book with text and illustrations called, *I Ching Meditations.* I began with a hand printed limited edition letterpress set of folders for the first three hexagrams. After completing that edition I continued with the illustrations in black and white pen and ink drawings for hexagrams one through sixteen. They were photocopied and published as a limited edition book. This was all before the birth of the Macintosh computer in January 1984. José Argüelles contributed a Foreword for that edition.

I discovered that in my moves across the country from Connecticut to California and back again twenty-three years later, along with several changes of computers, I had some how lost the original work that I had created in color digital format that I posted on a web page. I still have the low resolution of 72 dpi used for the web, but that resolution is not good enough for print.

After feeling stupid and horrified that I had lost all my high resolution work I accepted that fact and began again, creating all new images for hexagrams one through sixteen. Whenever I have switched the medium I am working in the process changes the outcome. On the positive side, I always like what I do better when I am forced to do it over again.

Another positive thing resulted from this loss is that now I am using graphic computer programs that allow me to create images at a faster rate than it took to do my original drawings. Having begun all these illustrations in hand cut woodblock prints and then in handset type on an antique letter press, the wonders of computer technology never cease to enrich and amaze me.

So ... I began my original graphic I Ching with woodcuts, a medium that originated in China. I Ching also originating in China, and was the first computer. So ... my She Ching is coming full circle here as she is created, produced and published via computer technology.

So what does all this have to do with how I arrived at *I Ching Prescriptions?* For one thing, I have been immersed in the varying processes of creating images that are inspired by the I Ching for a very long time now. While I am working on the images for my graphic interpretation, *I Ching Meditations*, I experience each hexagram as a whole, with the 6 lines as one continual process. When I am creating an image for each line I focus on one hexagram at a time. It is as if I had asked the I Ching a question and received all changing lines. I absorbed the meaning of each line as it related to the hexagram as a whole in a different way than when I asked a question and then read only the lines that changed.

The effect of creating illustrations for interpreting the meaning makes the experience of the I Ching more intense. As I live with a hexagram for a long time I become aware of the organic movement within the six lines contained within each situation. This process led me to the idea of choosing a situation for I Ching guidance rather than to only rely on the synchronistic method. I have read a number of I Ching articles on how to use the I Ching where the writer says to read **only** the lines that are changing for guidance. So I'm proposing a concept here with a different approach that goes against the traditional directions for consulting the I Ching. To give an example of the organic movement from one phase to another within the changing lines, I have included an example on page 92 that shows the development of movement within hexagram 10, *Treading,* excerpted from *I Ching Meditations.*

Choose Your Changes

When consulting the I Ching as a prescription, instead of asking a question in the traditional coin throwing approach, decide what issue in your life that you either want to deal with or are now involved in.

- Pick your prescription. Look at the list of the 64 Prescriptions on page 16 and 17. Decide what prescription you need. Look up the prescription distillation in this book, read it and see how the advice applies to your life.

- Each I Ching prescription has seven parts to it; the general meaning at the top and the six phases written from the bottom up. These lines are written on top of the image of a tinted color of the trigrams that create the hexagram.

- There are seven paragraphs of counsel for each hexagram prescription that can be used — one for each day of the week. Focus on or meditate on the prescription you have chosen. Keep a record over the next seven days as you follow each step. Write down what happens for you in the process.

ANOTHER WAY TO USE PRESCRIPTIONS

Suppose you are dealing with a situation where you feel that you are at a standstill. Look up hexagram number 12, *Standstill*. Read over all the lines which I have called *phases*. Notice that if you had cast the coins and actually received the hexagram for *Standstill* and had all the lines changed this would have turned into hexagram 11, *Peace*.

I've created a chart (page 18 - 19) of all the hexagrams and their opposites that shows what a hexagram transforms to if all the lines changed using a synchronistic method of consultation. Take the meaning to heart and see what happens if you act on the advice, rather than the more passive mode of asking the I Ching "what is . . .?" My idea is, why not act upon the I Ching philosophy the way one might by going to a therapist or doctor for help? You can decide what situation you want to be in rather than at a standstill and see what lines to emphasize to act or not act upon that will lead to a different situation. Be open to change. Of course, any hexagram can change into any other hexagram. Yes, the I Ching was the original computer.

To give just one example: Suppose you are in a state of standstill (#12) but you would like to be experiencing some enthusiasm (#16) instead.

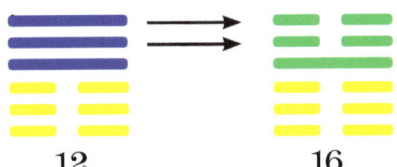

In order to get out of the Standstill and move to a situation of Enthusiasm the top two lines would need to be acted upon. Focus on the meaning of those lines and then see if you can bring about those changes to allow enthusiasm to happen. Use this same method for any of the 64 situations.

While creating the chart for the hexagrams of opposites when all lines are in movement I noticed a few things that caught my interest and something to ponder when choosing a change.

I'll give a few examples.

- If all the lines of hexagram 7, *The Army* change, the new hexagram becomes *Friendship.*
- Hexagram 53, *Development/Gradual Progress* speaks about the steps towards marriage. When all the lines change we get hexagram 54, The *Marrying Maiden* which is also about marriage but about the second wife
- *Approach*, hexagram 19 and *Retreat*, hexagram 33 are opposites.
- *Conflict*, hexagram 6, when lived out to the fullest becomes *Darkness*, hexagram 36.

Not all these transitions are equal in arresting my attention but some are worth noting.

Another way to approach the *I Ching Prescriptions* is with the traditional synchronistic way by throwing the coins, reading the changes, taking the advice, and then looking at the hexagram it changed into when you receive changing lines.

I Ching Prescriptions 1 — 32

☰	01. Creativity	☱	17. Following
☷	02. Receptivity	☶	18. Decay/Therapy
䷂	03. New Growth	䷒	19. Approach
䷃	04. Youthful Folly	䷓	20. Contemplation
䷄	05. Waiting	䷔	21. Biting Through
䷅	06. Conflict	䷕	22. Grace/Art
䷆	07. Army/Discipline	䷖	23. Splitting Apart
䷇	08. Union	䷗	24. Return
䷈	09. Many Small Things	䷘	25. Innocence
䷉	10. Treading/Conduct	䷙	26. Great Power
䷊	11. Peace	䷚	27. Nourishment
䷋	12. Standstill	䷛	28. Over Loaded/Crisis
䷌	13. Friendship	䷜	29. Abysmal Water
䷍	14. Wealth	䷝	30. Clinging Fire
䷎	15. Modesty	䷞	31. Influence
䷏	16. Enthusiasm	䷟	32. Duration/Marriage

I Ching Prescriptions 33 — 64

☷☰	33. Retreat	☱☲	49. Revolution
☳☰	34. Great Power	☲☴	50. The Cauldron
☲☷	35. Progress	☳☳	51. Shock
☷☲	36. In the Dark	☶☶	52. Keeping Still
☴☲	37. The Family/Clan	☴☶	53. Development
☲☱	38. Opposition	☳☱	54. The Second Wife
☵☶	39. Obstruction	☳☲	55. Abundance
☳☵	40. Deliverance	☲☶	56. The Wanderer
☶☱	41. Decrease	☴☴	57. Gentle Penetration
☴☳	42. Increase	☱☱	58. Joy
☱☰	43. Break-through	☴☵	59. Dispersion
☰☴	44. Coupling	☵☱	60. Limitation
☱☷	45. Gathering Together	☴☱	61. Inner Truth
☷☴	46. Pushing Upward	☳☶	62. Small Stuff
☱☵	47. Exhaustion	☵☲	63. After Completion
☵☴	48. The Well	☲☵	64. Before Completion

17

I Ching Chart for When All Lines Change

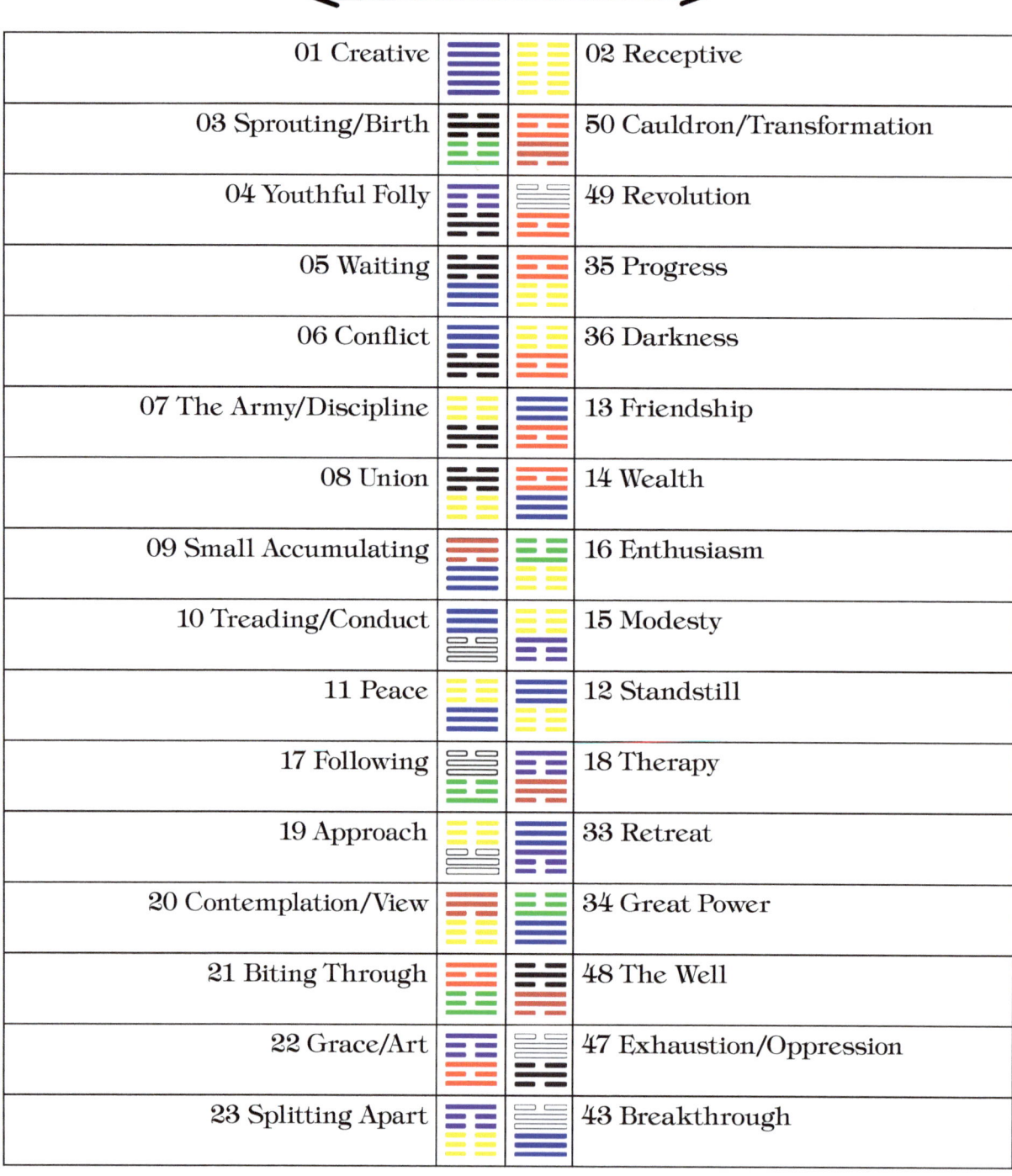

01 Creative			02 Receptive
03 Sprouting/Birth			50 Cauldron/Transformation
04 Youthful Folly			49 Revolution
05 Waiting			35 Progress
06 Conflict			36 Darkness
07 The Army/Discipline			13 Friendship
08 Union			14 Wealth
09 Small Accumulating			16 Enthusiasm
10 Treading/Conduct			15 Modesty
11 Peace			12 Standstill
17 Following			18 Therapy
19 Approach			33 Retreat
20 Contemplation/View			34 Great Power
21 Biting Through			48 The Well
22 Grace/Art			47 Exhaustion/Oppression
23 Splitting Apart			43 Breakthrough

I Ching Chart for When All Lines Change — P2

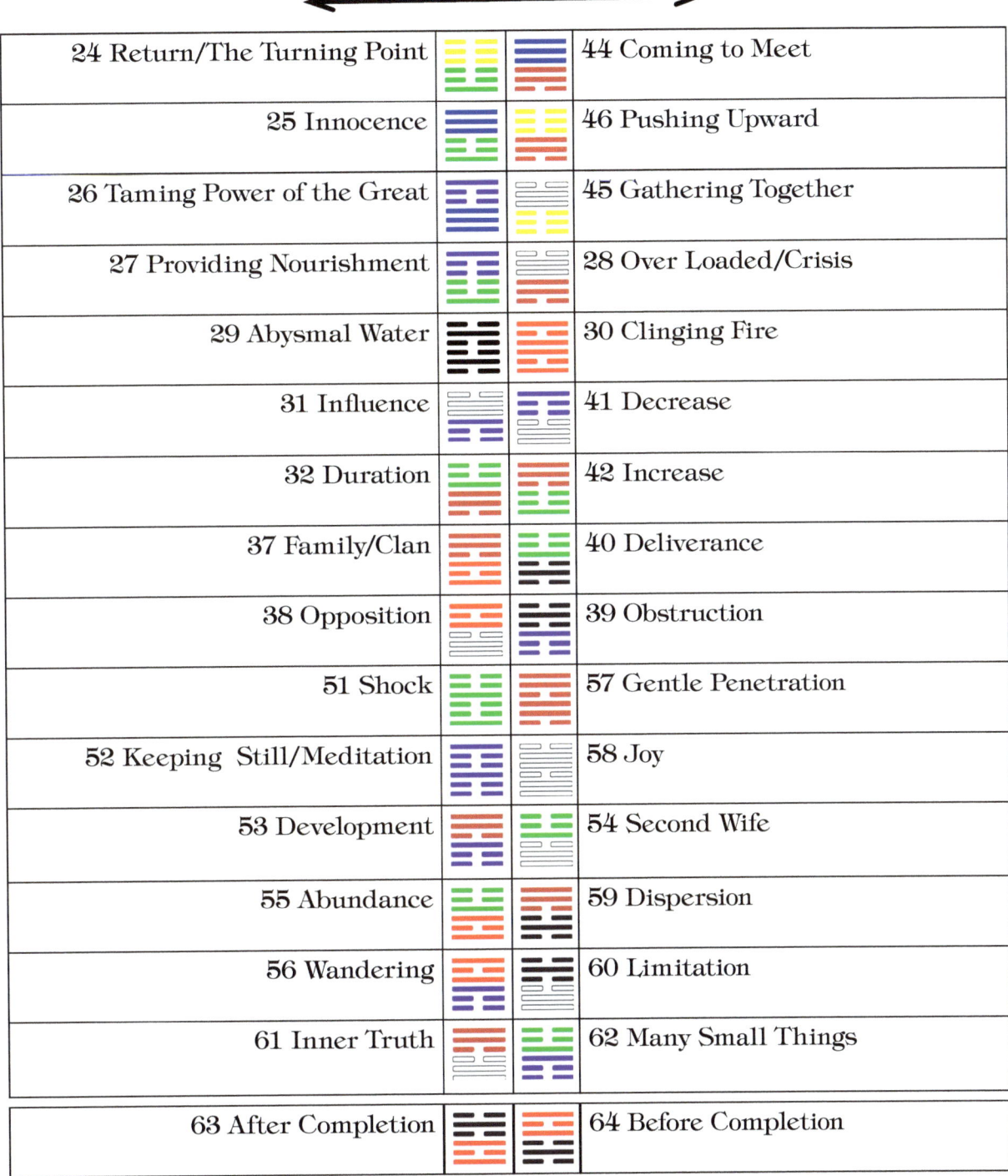

Trigram Language

by Rebecca Redfield

Each of the eight trigrams possesses a unique healing property. The Mountain trigram suggests a secure sense of self as a starting point of inquiry. The Wind/Wood trigram helps make us aware, available and able to participate in the process of life. Thunder brings attention to the moment. Lake is the capacity to witness all of creation without judgment. The Water trigram holds a transformation — from abyss-like longing to a lust for life. Similarly, Fire can feel clinging and friction, but opens to acceptance of it's surroundings. The Earth trigram teaches love and flexibility toward each other, and receptivity to the affection of others. Finally, realization of the Heaven trigram helps us accept that "What will be, will be!"

Subject and Object

The relationship between the upper and lower trigrams in a hexagram is often described as a subject/object relationship. The lower trigram represents the person inquiring of the I Ching, and the upper trigram represents that person's general environment, for example, people or institutions the person has to deal with.

The trigram language concept says: use subject and object to create a sentence. Each of the eight trigrams has its meaning as a subject and also as an object in a sentence. The result is a very basic sentence, the details of which are filled in according to the question that was asked when consulting the I Ching. Try out this very simple trigram language, and see what you think!

Trigram Language
by Rebecca Redfield

Lower Trigram		Meaning
Heaven	☰	Turning my will over to/Certain about . . .
Thunder	☳	Moment of . . .
Water	☵	Content with/Lust for . . .
Mountain	☶	Detailed examination /Noticing details of . . .
Earth	☷	Perfect acceptance of/Embracing . . .
WindWood	☴	Processing/Process of . . .
Fire	☲	Attention to . . .
Lake	☱	Appreciation of /Seeing /Containing . . .

Upper Trigram		Meaning
Heaven	☰	. . . God's will.
Thunder	☳	. . . the moment.
Water	☵	. . . lack/completion.
Mountain	☶	. . . stillness/detail.
Earth	☷	. . . God's love/love.
WindWood	☴	. . . miracle/God's process/growth.
Fire	☲	. . . knowledge/attention/objectivity.
Lake	☱	. . . knowledge/curiosity.

HEALTH QUESTIONS

In her book, *The I Ching and You,* Diana Ffarington Hook writes that asking questions relating to health are always difficult to answer. However she says that it is possible to diagnose correctly and that one should ask, *What is Wrong?* And then, *What is the Cure?* She says to look at what body parts the trigram refers to which will give you an idea of where the problem is or where the cure may be effected. The cause and the cure are not necessarily in the same place and that you may get an indication of the problem by studying the position of the moving line(s).

The chart on the next page describes the attributes associated with the trigrams which is useful for questions about health.

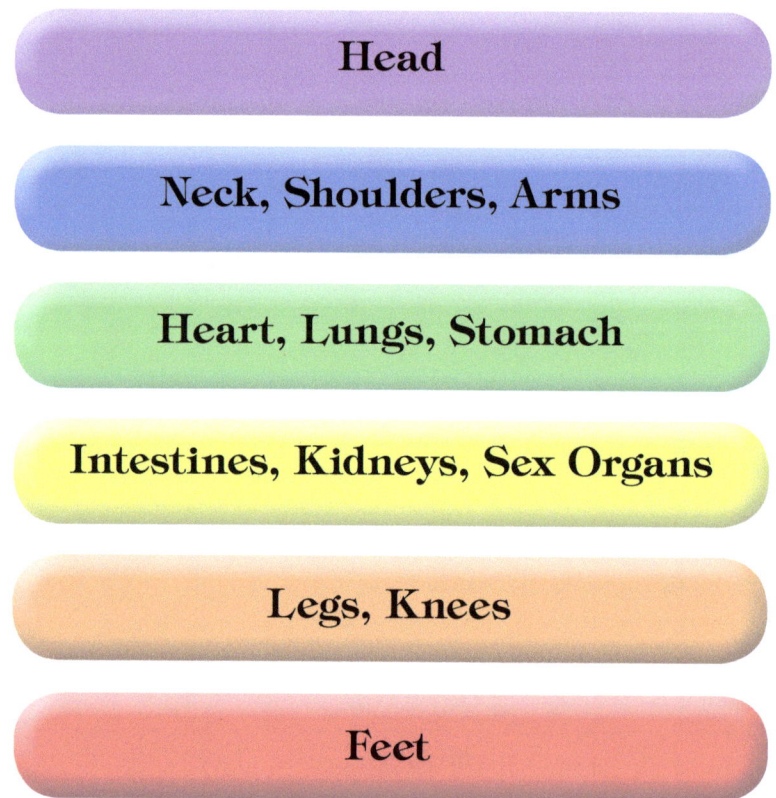

Trigrams Associated with the Body for Health Questions

Trigrams	Body
☰ Creative Heaven	Head, Male, Man's mind, Lean body, Strong body, Taking the lead.
☳ Arousing Thunder	Birth, Development, Electric, Expansion, Foot movement, Growth, Heart, Luxuriant growth, Movement, Music, Noise, Quick growing, Shocking into action, Sound, Starting things, Tears releasing tension, Violent.
☵ Abysmal Water	Anxiety, Blood, Danger, Deafness, Defected body, Difficulties, Distress of the mind, Ear, Earache, Flowing liquid, Melancholy, Moistening things, Penetrating, Sick in spirit, Water.
☶ Keeping Still Mountain	Fingers, Hands, Clutching hands, Ending of things, Gateways, Immovable, Obstruction, Openings, Perverse, Power of resistance, Protection from attacks, Stoppage, Stubborn, Sweetness.
☷ Receptive Earth	Female, Bearer of children, Blood.
☴ Gentle Wind & Wood	Air, Breath, Eyes, Grey hair, Odor, Thighs, White in the eyes, Wind.
☲ Clinging Fire	Eyes, Men with large bellies.
☱ Joyous Lake	Eating, Kissing, Laughing, Mouth, Smiling, Speech, Tasting, Tongue.

I Ching and Chakra Meditation

See page 96 and 99 for charts describing the arrangements of the trirams.

The Chakras

Chakra 7: Sahasrara (Universal Connection) is located at the crown of the head. Its color is white or violet and its issues are devotion, inspiration, selflessness and spiritual understanding.

Chakra 6: Ajna (Perception) is located between the eyebrows, just above the bridge if the nose. Its color is indigo blue and its issues are psychic, emotional and mental intelligence.

Chakra 5: Vissudha (purification) is located at the throat. Its color is bright blue. Its issues are communication, inspiration, expression and faith.

Chakra 4: Anahata (Love) is located at the heart, at the center of the chest). Its color is green and its issues are love, compassion, acceptance, and trust.

Chakra 3: Manipura (Power) is located at the solar plexus between belly button and bottom of the rib cage. Its color is yellow. Its issues are personalpower, self esteem, willfulness and energy.

Chakra 2: Svadhisthana (Sensual) is located at the lower abdomen between belly button and pubic bone. Its color is orange and its issues are sexuality, creativity, relationships and emotions. It connects us to others through feeling and desire.

Chakra 1: Muladhara (root) is located at the base of the spine. Its color is red. Its issues are survival, stability and self-sufficiency. It represents the element earth, instincts, and the physical plane.

The traditional method for consulting the I Ching is by throwing three coins six times or by dividing and counting yarrow stalks to arrive at an answer to a question. Allowing chance to provide an appropriate response to what is on your mind is a phenomenon that Carl Jung called synchronicity.

How to Toss Coins to Receive Your I Ching Hexagram

Chose 3 coins. They should all be the same size with a distinctly different front and back. The coins shown here are Chinese coins. You can use any kind of coin. Choose which side of the coin you designate as Yang and which as Yin. Yang is given a value of 3 and Yin the value of 2. Most instructions I have read say to designate heads to Yang and tails to Yin. I have also read where the opposite designation is prescribed. So choose what makes sense to you and then stick with that method.

Toss the 3 coins simultaneously letting them fall with no effort to control the outcome. Toss your 3 coins 6 successive times writing your answer from the bottom up.

The possibilities of receiving in each toss are values of 6, 7, 8 or 9. The even numbers 6 and 8 are Yin lines and odd numbers, 7 and 9 are Yang lines. If you receive all Yin, that equals 6 and is called a moving line, which changes to its opposite of Yang. If your coins equal the value of 9, that is a moving Yang line, changing to a Yin line. If you get a 6 or 9 moving line, make a mark on the line when you write it down (see examples below) so that when you go to look up what hexagram you received, you will know that the line or lines that changed into its opposite, now give you 2 hexagrams.

3 Heads (Yang) = 9 (changing)

3 Tails (Yin) = 6 (changing)

2 tails, one head (Yang) = 7 (not changing)

2 heads, one tail (Yin) = 8 (not changing)

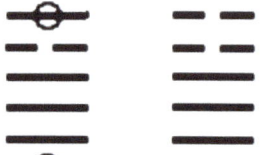

Here is an example of a coin toss with changing lines. hexagram 14 changes into hexagram 32 with the first and last Yang lines changing to Yin, thereby creating the second hexagram.

Hexagram Key Chart

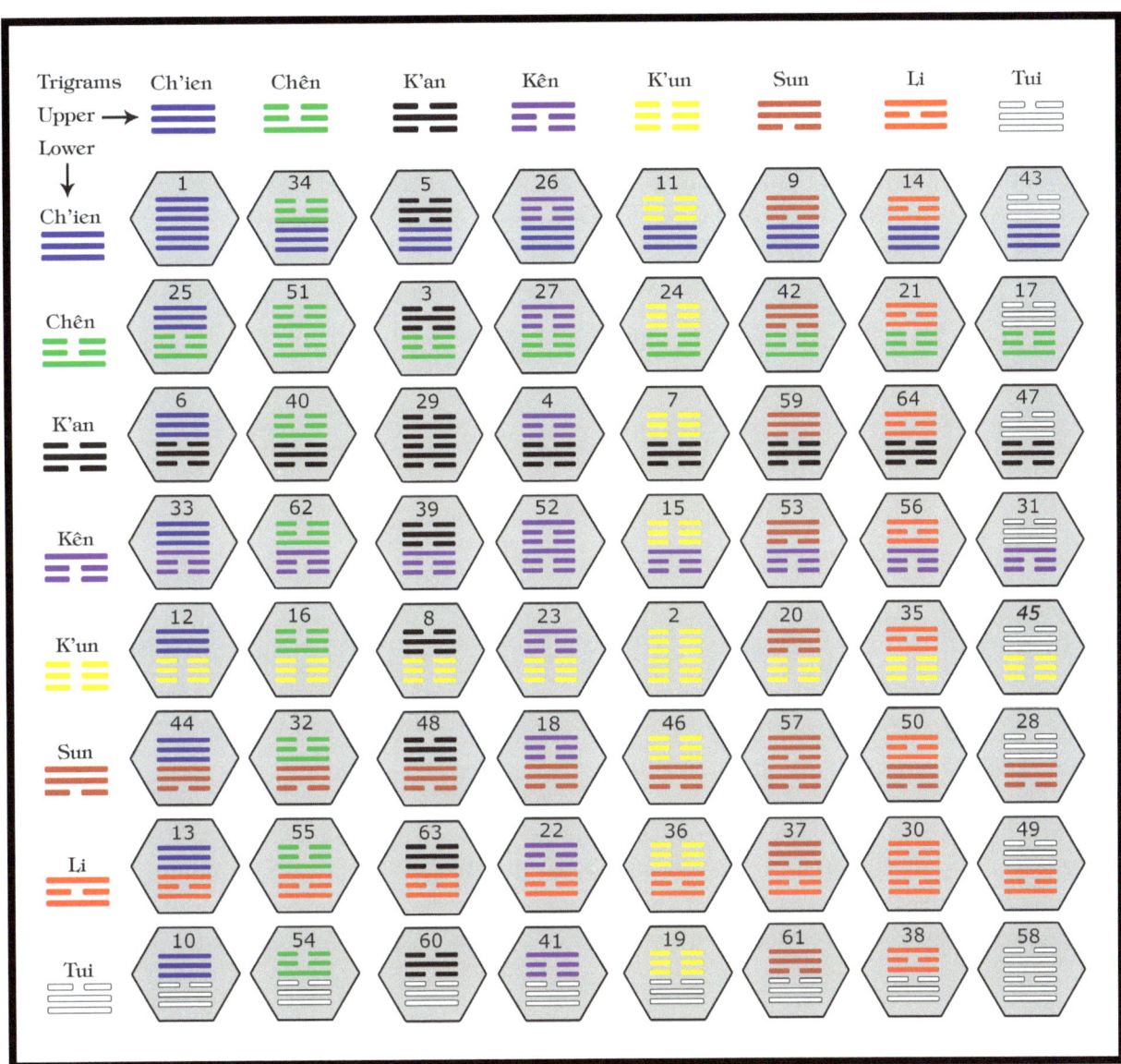

Prescription for *01. Creativity*

Heaven   then   Heaven

 *Ch'ien*

Creativity is a force that comes from beyond yourself, through yourself. Imagine that you are a pinpoint of light, a focal point of energy that originated in a galaxy beyond. Creativity originates in imagination.

Warning: When success comes be careful of ego inflation. After achieving fulfillment, if you are not careful, like Icarus, you may fly too high and fall.

Phase 6

As your creative work manifests recognition comes to you spreading your ideas like light over the world.

Phase 5

You have the choice to seek recognition in the world or remain by yourself. Only you know the right answer.

Phase 4

When you begin to get some recognition for your idea you will encounter distractions that can take you away from your original brilliant plan. Steel yourself against being influenced or interrupted by this possibility.

Phase 3

When the idea becomes clear in your mind seek a person or a place or a way to express it.

Phase 2

Incubate the idea. Obey the light inside. Do not force it. Ignore what others say. Do not expect recognition now.

Phase 1

The Six Phases ↑ of *Creativity*

Prescription for *02. Receptivity*

Earth   then   Earth

 *K'un*

Receptivity is the completion of creativity. Yield. Remain flexible. Be devoted to your ideas so that they will bloom. Honor your dreams. Nourish what you find there. Act like a mother giving birth. Protect. Respond. Let others take the lead for now.

Yield to your creativity. Don't fight it. Don't try to change anyone now. Remain open and accepting.

Phase 6

Be reliable, discrete, genuine, and solid like gold. Patience will be rewarded.

Phase 5

Remain reserved. Incubate. If necessary, hide for a while. Think of yourself like being pregnant. Something will be born.

Phase 4

Keep your work hidden for a while. Let things develop in their own time. Trust your process. Don't look for recognition now.

Phase 3

Be organized. Remain calm and follow your natural way of being in your own personal pattern. You possess within you now everything that you need.

Phase 2

Begin the work slowly, with caution. Let things solidify. While you can't walk on water you can when it turns to ice.

Phase 1

The Six Phases ↑ of *Receptivity*

Prescription for *03. Sprouting/Giving Birth*   Chun

Thunder then **Water**

Whether giving birth to a baby, a work of art, or growing a garden, the time is fraught with confusion, like a thunder and lightning rain storm. Separate what is necessary for you to do from the fear of doing it. Think of the seed of a tree sprouting into something that grows well beyond what you can see now. Chaos is part of the process. It is time to create order out of the confusion.

> Sometimes the difficulties may feel like they are too much to deal with. Do not succumb to feeling sorry for yourself. Continue with your creative task.

Phase 6

> You may be misunderstood by what you brought forth. Don't worry about that. Remain true to yourself and the truth wills out. You will eventually be rewarded.

Phase 5

> When you need help don't let pride get in the way to seek and then accept it. Be clear about what you need and how to attain it.

Phase 4

> Do not make the mistake of impulsively chasing something that is not your true nature.

Phase 3

> You may experience unexpected problems. Don't change direction. You will eventually find your way. Find a connection you feel comfortable with. Trust the process. Allow time to mature.

Phase 2

> Don't force anything before you are ready. Wait and get help however you may find it. Find a new group. Stick to your goal.

Phase 1

The Six Phases ↑ of *Sprouting/Giving Birth*

Prescription for *04. Youthful Folly*

Water then Mountain

 *Mêng*

It is not bad to look foolish when young. Making mistakes is part of the learning process. Don't pretend you know something when you do not. Be aware of your lack of knowledge and skills now and seek a good teacher to help you learn. Listen carefully so that you don't repeat your questions, thereby annoying and disrespecting your teacher. If you are the teacher, allow the pupil to come to you without interference.

Avoid a temptation that may lead you on the wrong path.

Phase 6

If you listen to your teacher, or one with more experience than you in the matter, you will be headed in the right direction for maturity.

Phase 5

While developing character don't get lost in unreal fantasies. If you are the teacher here, let the learner make and live with their mistakes and they will learn the hard way.

Phase 4

Do not be tempted to go beyond your abilities or take what does not belong to you. You will only get into trouble by indulging in either folly.

Phase 3

Be responsible, caring and kind. Treat all people equally. Develop character.

Phase 2

It is time for you to develop beyond seeming foolish. You need to apply a focused discipline to your learning. Try to enjoy this as a necessary part of the process to growth.

Phase 1

The Six Phases ↑ of *Youthful Folly*

Prescription for *05. Waiting*

Heaven then Water

 *Hsü*

Waiting is about accepting your fate. You can't make things happen before the time is ripe. While you are waiting face the truth of how things really are. During this period relax and enjoy yourself while you wait. Eat and drink, trusting that what you are waiting for will come.

Just when you think everything is hopeless and that what you have been waiting for is never going to happen, suddenly out of nowhere comes an unexpected turn of events. Good things come in sets of three.

Phase 6

Connect with kindred souls and share a meal. Maybe give a party and enjoy the moment. Have as much fun as you can during this time. Being positive about the wait will be more rewarding.

Phase 5

While waiting you may feel cut off and feel anxious. Relax. This is easier said than done but if you accept that you have no choice in the matter you will save yourself a lot of unnecessary angst.

Phase 4

Be careful. In your impatience you may become tempted to hurry things. Hold back this impulse or you will only attract the wrong events or wrong people.

Phase 3

You are becoming closer to the fate you are waiting for. People may be gossiping about you. You may have anxiety, fearing what you wait for will not happen. Stay calm. Ignore all bad vibes whether they come from inside yourself or from others.

Phase 2

You may feel anxious about something about to happen or you want to happen. Be patient. Write about what you want the outcome to be or paint a picture of it to meditate on.

Phase 1

The Six Phases ↑ of *Waiting*

Prescription for *06. Conflict*

Water then Heaven

 Sung

When a disagreement is brewing be sure to make your position clear without hostility. Seek justice without fear. Be on guard without getting involved with outside negativity. Meditation would help you now to keep a calm detachment from projections that may not be true.

If you insist on carrying on with this conflict you will never be free of it. You will be the loser even if you win. There is nothing to gain by having to be right all the time. Let it go.

Phase 6

Find an appropriate mediator to guide you through the conflict. Or you might meditate and let your unconscious guide to do the right thing.

Phase 5

Be clear about your point of view with confidence and retreat from the conflict. You will acquire peace by doing this.

Phase 4

When a conflict is about something that you own or created, whether intellectual property or a possession, no one can take away from you what belongs to you. Stop to think about the cause of the conflict.

Phase 3

If your opponent is stronger than you are, escape the situation now. Do not engage in the conflict that may bring problems to more than yourself in your community.

Phase 2

If you see a conflict on the horizon and can possibly avoid it make every effort to do so.

Phase 1

The Six Phases ↑ of *Conflict*

Prescription for *07. The Army/Discipline*

Water then Earth

 *Shih*

Take risks. Develop hidden potential. Be organized with a steady focus on your goal. You will need to sacrifice something in one area of your life to gain control in another. Be aware that if you over extend the use of control you will rebel against it.

After you win this particular battle for conquering a difficult goal you are able to teach others how to do this. Share what you have learned in this process of discipline for an attainable goal.

Phase 6

When you have made progress towards achieving your goal it is important to remain inspired. Do not allow a setback in behavior by thinking you will lose what you have gained in the quest for a new you in what ever field of discipline that you have battled with.

Phase 5

At times you will feel overwhelmed and have a set back in your present task of discipline. This is to be expected. Accept it and return to the task when you are ready.

Phase 4

Be inspired by your goal. Let it lead you. Don't allow old habits to take you off your path. Stay in control.

Phase 3

Act like a general. Take the orders you have defined to accomplish the task you have set. Reward yourself when you accomplish something towards achieving your goal.

Phase 2

Define your goal. Become organized. Be a leader. Understand the task needed to attain your goal.

Phase 1

The Six Phases ↑ of *The Army/Discipline*

Prescription for *08. Union*

Earth then Water

You may be surrounded by people and yet not feel connected to anyone. Be aware of the kind of people you want to be with. You may need to find a new group that reflects where you belong. Follow your heart. Be clear in yourself about who you are. You will attract the qualities that you manifest. If you find people you feel connected to, take the risk and join with them.

> When you find the right group of people don't hesitate to join them. If you let the opportunity go you will miss out on something valuable. On the other hand, if you find that you are in the wrong group leave it without hesitation.

Phase 6

> Don't try to convince anyone to join your group. Your force of character and personality shine. Those who belong know it and willingly join you without coercion. Remain open.

Phase 5

> When you find people that you feel connected to, openly demonstrate that feeling of union to them. You may become the leader of a new group.

Phase 4

> Don't bother wasting your time on those you know in your bones are not the right connections for you.

Phase 3

> You attract to you the people you are attracted to. You may become the center of a group.

Phase 2

> You will know when you find the right union for you. Be true to yourself and you will be recognized and welcomed. The truth of what you have to offer will be experienced in both directions.

Phase 1

The Six Phases of Union

Prescription for *09. Small Accumulating*

Heaven   then   Wind/Wood

 Hsiao Chu'u

This is the time when small things influence outcome. It is the moment before action, like waiting before the rain comes and seeing clouds in the distance. It is important to pay attention because even if you don't see the signs that point to what is coming, those events will influence what happens. If you can't influence what is to come be adaptable to what may cross your path at this time.

> Eventually all the little things that you have done in preparation will come to fruition. The moment will come like rain released from a cloud. If the result is not exactly what you had hoped for be content with what you have achieved.

Phase 6

> Find someone that you feel connected to in spirit. Sharing your mutual interests and supporting each other will be beneficial.

Phase 5

> When disagreements arise fighting can be dangerous and may bring about results you are not prepared for. If you are true to yourself and act with integrity this can be a time to act and move towards your goal.

Phase 4

> You may be stopped by an accident of fate. Or you may find yourself fighting with people you thought agreed with you. Stop. There is nothing one can do about that now. Be open and available to the right connection.

Phase 3

> Stick to your own personal path. Stay with the group that you know.

Phase 2

> You know what your true path is. Now return to following it.

Phase 1

The Six Phases ↑ of *Small Accumulating*

Prescription for *10. Treading/Conduct*

Lake then Heaven

 *Lü*

Learn how to act in the social world so you can get along and with people who may be or appear to be of higher social acceptance. Learn to get along with strangers. Use humor and good manners when managing the tiger who lives within you and the tiger who lives within others. Take a stand in your decisions.

Good conduct will reward you. Your power is in the process so if each step you take is with integrity the outcome will be successful and you will attain what you are striving for.

Phase 6

When you listen to your instincts yet are aware of any struggles that you may encounter you will have courage to proceed on a path that may at first seem difficult.

Phase 5

When you are on the right path you will know it. You will feel it. Go with the situation. Allow your instincts to guide you.

Phase 4

Don't fool yourself by thinking you can live beyond your means, whether physical, mental or financial. Don't get in over your head on any endeavor if you don't want to invite trouble.

Phase 3

Follow your instincts. Trust them. Don't become entangled in someone else's idea of what you should do. Don't ask for favors. Remain free.

Phase 2

Don't get caught up in obligations. Make no demands on others. Keep it simple. Find your own path with the goal of something worth while to strive for.

Phase 1

The Six Phases ↑ of *Treading/Conduct*

Prescription for *11. Peace*

Heaven then Earth  *T'ai*

Peace — Heaven on Earth and all are blessed. Peace is a time when people of all rank and place in society get along. This is a time of the soul in flower. You can be productive like Spring in bloom. Be content. Communicate your good fortune. Be generous, share the wealth and you will be at peace within.

The time will come when the state of peace will abandon you. This is just part of life's inevitabilities. Don't add to this fact with negativity. Accept what happens. Meditate. The cycle will change again.

Phase 6

Receptivity to your creativity brings a blossoming to the personality. When you listen to your heart you feel connected and peaceful. You experience a marriage of your innermost spirt enacted in life — a marriage of the opposites.

Phase 5

Honor and trust your heart's desire. Connect with those close to you in spirit. Allow your creativity to flower.

Phase 4

Change always happens. Night turns to day, riches to poverty, youth to old age. When the highs and lows happen remain centered. Remember during difficult times that they WILL change to the opposite. Don't identify with the drama.

Phase 3

Be gentle and kind with yourself. Be gentle and kind with people who may not be like you. Don't take a position of one extreme or the other. Walk the middle road.

Phase 2

Look around and find kindred souls, the people you belong with.

Phase 1

The Six Phases ↑ of *Peace*

Prescription for *12. Standstill*

Earth then **Heaven**

When everything comes to a standstill you may feel frustrated and uncomfortable. You may feel antisocial or forced into a separation. It is especially important to recognize your worth at this time. Don't succumb to feeling like a victim. Remain quiet. Don't waste energy on blaming yourself. Remember that trees grow in winter time when they are not in bloom. Think of the seed and all that it eventually becomes.

> When you are able to act again let go of any negative thoughts around the situation. Use your creativity to start the new process. Celebrate a new growth with that group of people you felt close to during the time of when you were in standstill.

Phase 6

> When you have been stopped for a while, eventually the light begins to dawn. Remain cautious yet without fear. A new situation emerges out of the old and you will see that standing still was necessary for a while.

Phase 5

> The time will come when your standstill begins to slowly change. Those people you surrounded yourself with at the beginning of the standstill may be closer and more connected to you now.

Phase 4

> Do not feel ashamed of having to standstill for a while. Pay attention to your dreams where the action is happening now.

Phase 3

> Trust this time as something necessary to experience for the larger picture of your life. No one said this was easy. Just remain open, be quiet and make plans while you are stopped for now.

Phase 2

> The first step to take in the time of Standstill is ironically the same as in the time of Peace. Look around and find kindred souls. Connect with those people where you feel you belong.

Phase 1

The Six Phases ↑ of *Standstill*

Prescription for *13. Friends in Community*      *T'ung Jên*

Fire then **Heaven**

Friendships develop when you unite with people who share an interest that reaches beyond the personal life. These friends share a common goal or ideal that transcends where or when you were born.

When the goal is to have friendship within a group it is important not to pair off in any kind of exclusivity that keeps others out.

Phase 6

If you have a disagreement that causes separation from a true friend, a gift of flowers is always understood as the blooming of true feeling. Those people who are connected by a deeper heartfelt reality can cry and then laugh again when they meet and see how silly their separation was.

Phase 5

There is always the possibility of quarreling within a group of friends. Let go of dissension. Remember to keep the ideals of the friendship in mind and work to preserve that. Confront the issues between you and work it out for the larger goal.

Phase 4

Mistrust can occur in a group of friends. Be on guard about this happening within yourself. Do not engage in any negativity that you might project onto others.

Phase 3

When you are in a community it can happen that not everyone will have the same goal or affinity. Accept that you may not feel connected to some in this group. You may feel detached at times. This does not mean that you don't belong there.

Phase 2

Join with a group of like-minded of people. This is the gateway to friendship. In order to maintain the integrity of the group don't hold back with secrets.

Phase 1

The Six Phases ↑ of *Friends in Community*

Prescription for *14. Wealth*

Heaven then Fire

 *Ta Yu*

Wealth is sometimes a matter of fate and is not measured only by material goods. You can be rich in ideas, creativity, inspiration or charity towards others. Allow your creativity to shine. Imagine the fire within you that radiates out to brighten the world. In order to gain wealth of any kind focus on one goal and then share the rewards. This will bring you riches beyond material pleasures.

When you are blessed from Heaven, your inner light shining, you help others just by revealing the integrity of your soul.

Phase 6

Remain true to yourself. When you really own something you can easily give it all away.

Phase 5

Know the difference between what is valuable to you and what is valuable to others. Sometimes people will be envious of what you have. So don't invite animosity by flaunting your wealth. Jealous people can be dangerous.

Phase 4

Serve others. Whether what you "own" is of a material or spiritual nature share it. You will receive much in the giving.

Phase 3

Define your plan. Strive to make your dreams and reality the same. If your goal is beyond your knowledge or capabilities, get help from responsible people who are strong in those skills you lack to help you to achieve what you want.

Phase 2

Begin with focus and hard work towards a desired goal. Be aware that your task is not always easy. Stick with it.

Phase 1

The Six Phases ↑ of *Wealth*

Prescription for *15. Modesty*

Mountain then Earth

 *Ch'ien*

There are situations where it is beneficial to be modest. All things change to their opposite over time. Be humble. Be simple. Keep things in balance. Don't take any extreme positions. Keep pride and ego out of the situation. Be polite and respectful. Trust your unconscious. Perhaps do something that connects you to the Earth.

Don't blame others for any difficulties that you may experience. Keep your ego out of it. If you are modest people will see and respond positively to this quality. If you don't complete what you set out to do, begin again.

Phase 6

Do what is needed with energy and good will. Do not brag about what you achieve. If you trust others they will in turn find you trustworthy. Modesty is not passivity.

Phase 5

Accept responsibility and do the work without expecting either reward or blame. Don't get trapped into an other's negativity. Remain true to your self. Let your actions speak for themselves.

Phase 4

Finish the task. Don't seek praise for your acts of good deed. Remain humble. People will appreciate you for your good work.

Phase 3

Speak from your heart. When this kind of sincerity and truth emanates from you without words it is felt by others.

Phase 2

Difficult tasks are made easier if you don't put off doing them. If you resist you only prolong and strengthen negativity towards the task. Assume nothing. Let your unconscious lead.

Phase 1

The Six Phases ↑ of *Modesty*

Prescription for *16. Enthusiasm*

Earth then Thunder

Be ready to respond spontaneously to any situation. Think like *"Thunder over the Earth"* — like a spring rain storm, sudden and refreshing. Be in the present moment. Go where the wind is blowing. Listen to or make music which will get you in touch with the divine. Dance and sing. Enjoy yourself and you will spread enthusiasm to all around you.

Sometime it is necessary to let go of enthusiasm so that you don't become exhausted for the wrong reasons.

Phase 6

Expect that sometimes your enthusiasm meets with resistance. When things become difficult is the exact time not to give up. Paint a picture, sing a song, dance to some music.

Phase 5

When you express sincere enthusiasm you draw others to you. Have no doubt that this will happen. Your sureness of action is catching. When your enthusiasm begins to wane you may be anxious. Rest for a while. Breathe.

Phase 4

When something comes your way that feels right for you do not doubt or hesitate. If you miss the right moment it will not come again. Act now!

Phase 3

Listen to the sounds from the past. Pay attention to what you learned. When you get the right message, go for it. When you feel things are not right, leave the situation. Act on your intuition.

Phase 2

Sometimes it is necessary to keep your enthusiasm to yourself.

Phase 1

The Six Phases ↑ of *Enthusiasm*

Prescription for *17. Following*

Thunder then Lake

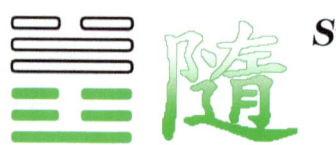 *Sui*

To acquire a following you first have to know how to follow. Learn a discipline and become expert at it. Add your own touch of what you learned to make the skill new. Then teach what you learned to the people who are following you. Take one step at a time. Adapt and take a rest when necessary.

> In the process of following and being followed after you become a sage in your field and put it behind you, a next generation follower may appear and once more you begin the process again. Who is following whom?

Phase 6

> Follow your soul, follow your heart. You will attract followers after you have been a follower with much devotion. You will attract what you seek and love and serve, thereby creating a perfect circle of following.

Phase 5

> If you acquire a following you may attract people who are not sincere or truthful and have their own agenda in mind. Be wary of false flattery.

Phase 4

> When you follow a new path or new group it is inevitable that you will leave some people behind. They may not be able to relate to what you are doing. Go after what you want and don't worry about those who don't approve or understand.

Phase 3

> You might have to separate from friends who don't approve of your new plan. Let them go and stick to your decision. Find people who support what you are doing now.

Phase 2

> Forget about what you thought you knew and be open to a new way. If you are a leader with a following pay attention and be responsive to those learning from you. Keep your principals about your skill but keep an open mind so that you can also learn from the learners.

Phase 1

The Six Phases ↑ of *Following*

Prescription for *18. Corruption/Therapy*

Wind/Wood then **Mountain**

Ku

If you feel poisoned or abused by the acts of your parents the situation can feel like a can of worms. Don't feel guilty. Get help and work on the issue with focus. You can succeed. Cautiously and with consciousness start a new beginning. It will take some time. Avoid relapse by removing the cause for the decay. Nourish a new growth cycle.

> At some point it will be time to let go of the past. Have high aspirations. Strive to achieve a universal goal for the good of all that goes beyond the limitations that you were born into.

Phase 6

> You may feel like you don't have the strength to handle the corruption of the past and are tempted to submit to accepting what was. Deal with it. Find a new way.

Phase 5

> Have good intentions as you put more energy into working on father or authority issues. Try acting as if you had a good authority figure to grow up with. Conditions will improve slowly. Be patient. Be the person you want to be.

Phase 4

> By getting help you can heal past authority father figure issues. You can be successful by reforming your own behavior. Begin again. Find your own purpose in life.

Phase 3

> Work on mother issues. Be gentle about taking care not to wound in the process. When dealing with issues of lack of nurturing find the source before trying to change anything.

Phase 2

> Look at what may have gone wrong with the past relationship with your father. It may not be his fault. The problem could have begun with grandparents and was handed down through generations. Heal this past decay to build a better future not only for yourself but for your children. End the cycle.

Phase 1

The Six Phases↑ of *Corruption/Therapy*

Prescription for *19. Approach*

Lake then Earth

 Lin

When you reach out to approach be like Spring time. Make contact with love. Be joyous and hopeful. Be sympathetic, open, gracious, and consistent. Welcome those who approach you without expectations. Be inviting, tolerant, protective and inspiring. Don't rush things. Teach those who look to you for guidance. You are blessed to share. Make use of the time while it lasts.

> Even if you feel you have no more need for involvement, be magnanimous and help others. Be generous and honest with inner determination. You will get what you need.

Phase 6

> Approach or allow for being approached without prejudice. Give of yourself with an open mind. Act with maturity to achieve success.

Phase 5

> While things are going well in your approach don't take your success for granted. If you make a mistake, own it and make up for it.

Phase 4

> When you approach be wise in your behavior. Take the lead. Choose the right people to approach.

Phase 3

> When you are approaching or being approached remember that even though in the law of change things always transform to their opposites that you are doing the right thing now. When you are approached by kindred spirits you feel and know that this is a fated encounter.

Phase 2

> Cooperate and join with others. Focus your mind and heart with determination. Don't doubt.

Phase 1

The Six Phases ↑ of *Approach*

Prescription for *20. Contemplation/Viewing*   觀   *Kuan*

Earth then **Wind/Wood**

Be like a tower with a wide view from a mountain top where you can see and be seen from a distance. Remain centered while viewing the broader picture and you will become wise and learn the mysteries of life. You will become an example for others to emulate like a tower of an ideal. By contemplating the laws of the universe you will influence others and will effect them without their being aware of your power. Contemplation while penetrating the meaning of the situation is a sacred time.

> Look at your life again. Keep your ego out of it. Contemplate with your heart. View the effect your actions have had on your life and in turn effected others. All those you were associated with also had their affect on you. Think about that.

Phase 6

> Look back at your life experiences and contemplate what kind of effect you have had on others. When this has been good you will feel content and satisfied with how you have lived your life.

Phase 5

> You may find yourself invited as an honored guest. Act with authority so that you can be a positive influence. You will enjoy that special place when you have earned it.

Phase 4

> Contemplate what your circumstances were at birth and where you are now. Think about the effect you have on others and you will know if you are making the right decisions.

Phase 3

> We tend to view everything from our own limited perspective. Work on having a larger understanding of what you see and experience.

Phase 2

> In the beginning of contemplating or observing, especially if you are young, you may not understand the larger picture or the broader view of things.

Phase 1

The Six Phases ↑ of *Contemplation*

Prescription for *21. Biting Through*  Shih Ho

Thunder then Fire

Watch out for people who are not telling the truth. Look for what is not obvious. Find the truth by slowly nibbling at the facts. Confront the issue with determination while remaining respectful. Bite through the obstacles with energy. Act with the force of thunder and lightning! Clear the air. Remove what is unnecessary. Be clear when enforcing the law with your judgement.

> Some people are incorrigible. They don't listen to counsel. They don't understand what happened. If you cannot learn from your mistakes you lose friends and achieve nothing.

Phase 6

> Sometimes you can be lenient with punishment. Confront all past issues with your family. Be aware of responsibility in the matter so you don't make a mistake. Follow the golden rule and don't seek revenge.

Phase 5

> Take direct action and be firm in the discipline for the punishment prescribed. This work will feel tiresome, like boring drudgery. Do it anyway. The end result will be for everyone's benefit.

Phase 4

> When dealing with an old problem that has become poisonous a punishment is necessary. You are the right person for that job. You have to do it.

Phase 3

> When you encounter a situation when some one has wronged you take corrective action. Bite through the obstacles with decisiveness and take the upper hand.

Phase 2

> When you feel locked up you may do things that you come to regret. Correct these little mistakes before you make bigger ones.

Phase 1

The Six Phases ↑ of *Biting Through*

Prescription for *22. Grace/Adornment*

Fire then **Mountain**   賁 *Pi*

The world of art is about the beauty of form and decoration. Show your inner beauty with tranquility reflected in radiance. Cultivate the ability to enjoy life with grace and elegance.

Perfect grace is where ornamentation and decoration are not needed.

Phase 6

When you find some one to express and share your joy of life with you may want to offer a gift. Sincerity of feeling now is more important than how much you spend. Your true love understands and does not want more than this.

Phase 5

In this beautiful situation you might find your true love inspired by mutual thoughts that transcend time and space.

Phase 4

Celebrate art with friends and find yourself in a charming situation, drinking wine and feeling mellow. Don't over do it.

Phase 3

Don't be vain. You might let your hair grow or get a new hair style but don't think that this replaces beauty within. Maintain integrity. Form is a result of content.

Phase 2

Don't pretend to be more than you are. Be open to what needs to be done now.

Phase 1

The Six Phases ↑ of *Grace/Adornment*

Prescription for *23. Splitting Apart*

Earth   then   Mountain

When the roof collapses submit to fate. When the situation can't support what is rotten you will need to sacrifice. This is the end of a cycle. This is the time to get rid of bad habits. Removing old skin enables and reveals a renewal. When separating from the present situation you will feel a loss of direction. Go outside and prune the trees while you prepare to adapt to new growth.

> The seed of all that was good in the situation remains while the rest falls away. Evil destroys itself. Integrity wins. Eliminate all that is outdated and use what is left for the new beginning. Celebrate with some ceremonious ripe fruit.

Phase 6

> Don't rely on pre-conceived plans. Allow your self to receive help from women or the feminine energy. This is the end of a cycle and the new time coming can be powerful.

Phase 5

> The situation cannot be avoided. Have courage. Let it go. Remain quiet.

Phase 4

> Be careful that you don't lose contact with those who matter to you. Remain loyal to those you know are truly connected and ignore the rest. Be decisive.

Phase 3

> Don't remain in denial about what is happening. You need help. Be careful. Know who your friends are. Don't become isolated. Have a clear and strong purpose.

Phase 2

> Eliminate evil people or those who are disloyal. Get rid of what is not working in your life. As a symbolic gesture for your first step, change the sheets on your bed or even trade it in for a new one.

Phase 1

The Six Phases ↑ of *Splitting Apart*

Prescription for *24. Return/The Turning Point*  *Fu*

Thunder then Earth

After things have split apart they return to a new form. This is a return of the spirit; a return of life. This is like the time of the winter solstice when the light begins to return. This is the way of nature. Discard the old. Go in the opposite direction or have a rebirth and go back to the beginning. Become who you are meant to be. Embrace a new field in a new cycle. Think of yourself like a tree with deep roots, resting in winter time and then leaves budding again in the spring.

Don't be deluded or deceived by making the mistake of going back to the old ways. You will then miss this new opportunity and it will take years of recovery when missing the right time to act.

Phase 6

Destroy the old ways to enjoy this new time. Victory! Enjoy a change of attitude. Be magnanimous.

Phase 5

You may have to go on alone. Go your own way. Don't be led astray.

Phase 4

Returning to your true self may be difficult but don't even think about going back. Use willpower.

Phase 3

Relax and enjoy being with people of like mind.

Phase 2

Let go of any pain caused by previous splitting. Make adjustments for a new way.

Phase 1

The Six Phases ↑ of *Return/The Turning Point*

Prescription for *25. Innocence*

Thunder then Heaven

 *Wu Wang*

Have no ulterior motives. Remain true to your natural child-like spirit. Act with spontaneity and confidence and at the same time try not to be impulsive. Remain constantly aware and when necessary correct things as they happen.

When the timing isn't right do not try to push fate. Let go of the plan for now. Wait with patience for a better opportunity.

Phase 6

Do every task for its own sake without looking to the result and it will turn out well. Flowers bloom when they are ready.

Phase 5

Pay attention and be on guard for unexpected events. If something of value should be taken from you let it go. Maybe you did not need it.

Phase 4

Don't worry. You can't lose what belongs to you. Follow your own path by doing what is right. Maintain integrity.

Phase 3

If an unfortunate event happens that you did not cause, let nature take its course. Things will get better by themselves. Use your imagination and envision things the way you want them to be.

Phase 2

Remain innocencent keeping an open heart.

Phase 1

The Six Phases ↑ of *Innocence*

Prescription for *26. Accumulating Great Power*

Heaven   then   Mountain

You can accumulate powers with three kinds of "holding firm." Hold back, hold together and hold as in nourishing. You have hidden treasures. Celebrate a festive meal with your family. Look at your family tree history and note what these people have done that you may have inherited. Decide what is valuable. Realize your potential. Be persistent. Repetition of good habits will keep you strong. Be active in the community. Earn money outside the home.

> After accumulating great energy have no doubt about getting what you worked for. You deserve it.

Phase 6

> When you have confronted and then eliminated powerful obstacles you will move forward with ease and be successful.

Phase 5

> By confronting head on any difficult obstacles in the way to your success you will become stronger.

Phase 4

> Stick to your plan. Hard work will bring you what you want. Remain cautious. The way is open if you have the skill to go forward and be protected from what you can't anticipate ahead of time.

Phase 3

> You may feel held back for reasons that you cannot control. Wait and store energy for when the time is right.

Phase 2

> Drop any negativity you may have from the past, whether from your own experience or from your ancestors. Don't take action yet.

Phase 1

The Six Phases of *Accumulating Great Power*

Prescription for *27. Providing Nourishment*

Thunder then Mountain

You learn a lot about a person by noticing what they regard as important to nourish. Be mindful of how you nourish yourself. Keep things in proper measure for balance. You need both material and spiritual nourishment. Be careful of the words that come out of your mouth. Do they nourish others? Examine your past ways of nourishing so that you can make the correct choices in the future. Nourish new experience.

> After you absorb nourishment from past experience drink it in. You can then enjoy using this knowledge to help others with responsibility in providing nourishment.

Phase 6

> If you go off your diet or are upset by negative words regarding either giving or receiving nourishment get help from a spiritual advisor. Don't try to go beyond what you can do.

Phase 5

> Find the right people and place to share your nourishment. What is the best way to help them?

Phase 4

> If you seek nourishment from something that does not nourish, you will pay the price for a long time. Give and receive real nourishment.

Phase 3

> Do not depend on others for your nourishment. If you can't support yourself for the nourishment that you need you will be very uncomfortable. Maintain discipline.

Phase 2

> Do not envy others who appear to have more than you. Don't leave things up to chance. Take control. Be self-reliant.

Phase 1

 54   The Six Phases  of *Providing Nourishment*

Prescription for *28. Over Loaded/Crisis*  Ta Kuo

Wind/Wood then Lake

Crisis! You are over burdened or in over your head. Leave the situation quickly. When structure dissolves this is ime for a transition. Let go of the past and move beyond it. Stand by what you know is true and have the strength to stand alone. When you are forced to push beyond limits for a purpose that you believe in you must be strong and courageous and then accept what happens.

Danger. If you get in over your head you could be swept away. Sometimes the sacrifice is necessary.

Phase 6

You may have a renewing burst of energy. Enjoy this while it lasts.

Phase 5

After living through the transition you feel strong. Rest. Don't push further than is necessary now.

Phase 4

A sacrifice of the old to begin the new brings a collapse under the weight of the burden. What now?

Phase 3

Get a new perspective in a new start. A spurt of energy will release extraordinary growth needed to make the transition. Find someone to cooperate with you.

Phase 2

Lay the foundation for a new move. Prepare for the change carefully. Be clear about your intent.

Phase 1

The Six Phases ↑ of *Over Loaded*

Prescription for *29. The Abysmal Water*

Water then Water

 *K'an*

The ancient Chinese thought of water as the symbol for the heart, the soul locked in the body. Water is the image of light yang within the dark yin, signifying reason. This is a critical time for confronting dangerous situations and taking risks. You have no choice. Keep an objective point of view. Penetrate the meaning of the situation and take action for correction. Confront your fears and develop character. Be like water and flow around obstacles. Reach your goal step by step with constant practice and repetition. Don't avoid any task. Remain true to yourself. Teach and learn.

When you are so afraid that you become reckless in behavior you will become lost with no hope of escape and be imprisoned in this pit of danger.

Phase 6

When things are just beginning to ease up do what is easy and natural. Move like water by simply flowing on.

Phase 5

Remain calm. The trouble is not your fault. Keep an open mind. Have a glass of wine while you wait it out.

Phase 4

When you find yourself with a lot to handle thrashing around in fear will get you into deeper trouble. Wait and do nothing for a while.

Phase 3

When you find yourself in danger with trouble on all sides, do not attempt to escape. Remain calm and try not to become overwhelmed. Take small steps to find your way out.

Phase 2

When you become used to being submerged in danger you can become part of it and find yourself lost. Don't become trapped in depression.

Phase 1

 56

The Six Phases ↑ of *The Abysmal Water*

Prescription for *30. The Clinging Fire*

Fire then Fire

This is a time of interlocking cycles. You have the concentrated energy of a doubled fire burning with clear inner and outer light radiating in all directions. Fire must cling to something in order to burn. Acknowledge your need to depend on something to keep on shining. Cling to what is the correct action. Articulate. Illuminate. Discriminate. And while doing all that try not to get burnt out.

When you have to deal with a disappointment do it willingly. Eliminate bad habits that get in the way of clarity of mind and in so doing don't be too hard on yourself while living through the experience.

Phase 6

When you lose a friend or a place in your life and you feel sad let your feelings be known. Cry and let it all hang out. Accept that life does come to an end for all.

Phase 5

Moving too fast, like a meteor that burns quickly and dies out, will cause you to fall. Let go of what you can't do or can't use.

Phase 4

In the light of the setting sun don't get stuck in the past. Don't piss and moan and feel sorry for yourself when things don't go the way you want. Everything is temporary and transitory. Enjoy life while you can. Live in the moment.

Phase 3

In the yellow light of midday peruse culture. Create some art.

Phase 2

In the beginning of morning light respect your path and make the right decision. Your first steps will influence all that follows. Have clarity of mind with clearly defined motives. Learn to see in the dark.

Phase 1

The Six Phases of *The Clinging Fire*

Prescription for *31. Influence/Courtship*

 Hsien

Mountain then Lake

This is a time of harmony between Yin and Yang energy within yourself and with those you may meet. Listen to your intuition and allow yourself to be influenced to join with another in relationship. When there is strong mutual attraction that includes a spiritual dimension you know that you belong together. You will be approached when you are receptive to that possibility.

> Empty talk will not influence anyone.

Phase 6

> The unconscious mind has more effect on your actions than what you think or say. You can't change this. In order to influence you must be open to being influenced.

Phase 5

> Don't try to influence people. Let your inner vibrations be the attraction. It is not always what you say that influences others but how you act and who you are intrinsically that radiates out and permeates the atmosphere. Don't be afraid of your new feelings. The heart speaks with sincerity.

Phase 4

> Don't spend time going after everyone who crosses your path. Think before you act. Be sure. Wait and see. Stay independent for a while.

Phase 3

> Wait until you are motivated to action by something real. Don't be impulsive. Let it happen.

Phase 2

> You may feel an attraction that is not yet noticed by the other. Proceed with awareness of the spiritual influence.

Phase 1

 58

The Six Phases ↑ of *Influence/Courtship*

Prescription for *32. Duration/Marriage*

Wind/Wood then Thunder

 Hêng

Duration is self-contained and self-renewing; a new beginning at every ending; continual movement within fixed laws of a cycle. Be aware that as times change, you must change with them. Marriage endures when you do not run away when troubles erupt. Be constant. Rituals and symbols help guide you to keep what you have pledged to last. Make a symbol for endurance. Paint a picture, write a poem, compose a song. Seeing the symbol aids in keeping the commitment. Find your path and stick to it.

Restlessness prevents duration. You cannot force commitment. It is there or it isn't. Find your way.

Phase 6

If things have gone badly, do you want to correct the situation? Decide if you can and if it is worth it. Sometimes it is best to stick to traditional ways, other times one must be flexible to keep the partnership.

Phase 5

When things go badly in a relationship the problem can come from outside or may stem from within yourself. If you don't feel connected it may be time to leave. Don't expect to find something that was never there.

Phase 4

Do not go back on your word. Don't betray yourself. Don't be swayed by moods of negativity and don't always blame externals. Develop character.

Phase 3

Don't be afraid to push beyond what you think is possible now. Commit to the situation. Treat your partner the way you want to be treated in return.

Phase 2

In the beginning relationships need to develop and mature. Something that lasts long begins gradually.

Phase 1

The Six Phases↑ of *Duration/Marriage*

Prescription for *33. Retreat*

Mountain then Heaven  Tun

Some times a retreat is necessary and not to be thought of as weakness. Retreat can be a strengthening, saving energy to use at the right time rather than struggle with what simply wears you out. Retreat in your mind from those who show animosity. Don't give away your energy on a situation that wastes your precious time.

Don't doubt your decision. Remain detached and content with your retreat.

Phase 6

Stick with your decision to leave the situation. Choose the right time to retreat in friendliness. Be a good example.

Phase 5

Accept the need to retreat and adjust to the circumstances. Let go of people that you need to be free of and stay connected with those who matter to you.

Phase 4

When you are held back from being able to retreat you feel a lack of freedom. When a person insists on remaining connected you might have to keep them around so that they do not become a dangerous enemy. This is a difficult pill to swallow but sometimes necessary.

Phase 3

When those we are retreating from won't let go you can retreat from them within your mind.

Phase 2

Keep still in your mind and your actions. Remain patient and calm. Get ready with a new plan of action.

Phase 1

The Six Phases ↑ of *Retreat*

Prescription for *34. Great Power*

Heaven then **Thunder**

 *Ta Chuang*

When manifesting great strength it is important to be aware of how you use your power. Take direct decisive action combined with wisdom and strength. Do not use excessive force. The power of inner strength includes justice and integrity.

Sometimes you make mistakes. This is the time for hard work. Learn what you did wrong. Fix the problem and the way will become clear.

Phase 6

When you encounter an obstacle be sure to use your mind and not brute force. Then all goes well.

Phase 5

Do what you can now. Don't hold back. And at the same time don't over do it. You will arrive at a place with no more problems.

Phase 4

Do not use brute force. Confront past problems. Don't boast about strength or power. Use your heart in the matter.

Phase 3

Find the right path and begin moving forward. Don't get over confident at this phase of the process.

Phase 2

Don't do anything rash. Begin slowly. Use care in your movement.

Phase 1

The Six Phases↑ of *Great Power*

Prescription for *35. Progress/Flourishing*  Chin

Earth then Fire

Imagine yourself to be like the image of the sun rising slowly over the Earth helping everything to grow. Accept recognition. It is a time when you will prosper and progress with ease. Trust that you will be guided with clarity to not misuse your power or influence. Socialize while you give and receive.

Don't associate with people who are of no help to you. They will waste your time. It is always beneficial to work on your own self-improvement.

Phase 6

Win or lose, it doesn't matter. If you made best use of your abilities you will eventually be rewarded. Everything happens at the right time.

Phase 5

Use integrity. Don't pursue the superficial. Be wary of people who don't have your interest at heart.

Phase 4

The help of others is appreciated as you continue with the process of progress. Help others now as well. Be like the sun that shines everywhere. Don't hide your generous spirit.

Phase 3

If you are slowed down in progress, don't get depressed or anxious. You will attract someone who is like minded who will help you with your task.

Phase 2

In the beginning you may not feel sure about your direction and fear making a mistake. Proceed with good intentions. Don't worry, all is for the good.

Phase 1

The Six Phases ↑ of *Progress/Flourishing*

Prescription for *36. Darkening of the Light*   明夷   *Ming I*

Fire   then   Earth

When the sun slips beneath the horizon we have darkness. You may be feeling darkness within. Darkness is often an act of fate, not something that happens through your own fault. Accept what is. During this time of being in the dark it will be necessary to do something very difficult by using force of will. This is a time for clairvoyance and inner vision. No matter how painful the situation, keep your inner light as the way to experience enlightenment. You can be an inspiration to others now. Rest.

When the dark time is finally over think back to how this situatioon began? What did you learn from it? Are you feeling free from that depression now?

Phase 6

You may have been hiding for a while, keeping your depression to yourself, or pretending things were alright. The situation changes when you face what you were imprisoned by. Relief!

Phase 5

Leave depression behind now. Find the heart of the darkness and perhaps allow feelings of anger to arise and be released. The new light is slowly emerging.

Phase 4

During this time of darkness remain calm in meditation and you will reach a point of release. Your heart will open to discover what you can see in the dark.

Phase 3

You feel wounded in spirit and are hindered by the wounding. The healing process requires you to shine your light inside with your true spirit by helping others now.

Phase 2

You might go on a diet or fast during this time. Meditate. Trust what is happening even if you don't know the result. Expect that there will be those who do not understand. Let them go.

Phase 1

The Six Phases ↑ of *Darkening of the Light*

Prescription for *37. The Family/The Clan* 家人 *Chia Jên*

Fire then **Wind/Wood**

The family is society in nuclear scale, proceeding outward to influence the larger culture. It is important that all in the clan get along. How you behave in this context affects the clan as a whole. Learn about the customs of the society you live in. Establish correct relationships according to these customs. Use yin/feminine energy to take care of all that happens inside the place where you live. Use yang/masculine energy to deal with the outside world. Everyone within the clan has a specific responsibility.

The atmosphere in the family depends on the character of the person who maintains the home. Assume responsibility and the home will flourish.

Phase 6

The father figure in the family should act like a benevolent king of good character who builds trust. Do not make yourself feared. Act from the heart and give affection.

Phase 5

Being of service in the clan is helpful and appreciated. This creates happiness and well being within the family unit.

Phase 4

Take charge. Stick with and enforce the rules. Confront issues when they arise so that they don't grow larger and become unmanageable. Balance discipline. Don't lose your temper or be too severe when problems arise.

Phase 3

Feminine energy is in charge of social obligations as well as the important task of providing food and nourishment for the family. Don't try to lead the group. Keep within the specified mores of the clan.

Phase 2

Stay within the home and prepare for what is necessary to create the family unit. Make rules of order. Know what your responsibility is and stick with it.

Phase 1

The Six Phases ↑ of *The Family/The Clan*

Prescription for 38. Opposition

Lake then Fire

K'uei

What opposition do you have to contend with now? You may feel like you are in unfamiliar territory. Do you have a conflict between your inner feelings and outward expression? Be flexible and open to new situations or chance meetings. When opposing forces in human interaction or nature are integrated they can be powerful. Retain your individuality in such an encounter while maximizing the powers of both sides to form a creative solution.

Sometimes you may reject the very people who want to be your friend and help in this opposition. Was there a misunderstanding? Don't let past hurts run your life now. Be open and accepting. Opposition will disappear.

Phase 6

After struggling with negative feelings because you are being excluded by opposing forces, the strengths that you inherited will lead the way. You meet sincerity of connection coming from outside yourself, forming a completion in the meeting of opposites.

Phase 5

Get in touch with the force that nourishes you. You might meet this energy in another person or you may find it within. Your heart knows the truth and leads the way.

Phase 4

If you are stopped for reasons out of your control you may feel unable to proceed with your plan. Don't accelerate the issue of opposition now. Stick to your plan while you wait for things to become clear as to how to proceed.

Phase 3

When you let go of fighting the opposing forces and accept them you will find a soul connection in surprising circumstances. When you are open to that possibility of connection, it will happen.

Phase 2

If you lose a friendship don't waste time trying to recapture it. Stay in the present. When you feel opposition don't combat it head on. Wait and the negativity will resolve itself out of the truth of the underlying need for each other.

Phase 1

The Six Phases ↑ of *Opposition*

Prescription for *39. Obstruction/Limping*

Mountain then Water  Chien

Does it feel like you are stuck between a rock and a hard place? Proceed carefully. Don't try to push through the obstruction directly. Don't exaggerate the problem. Be adaptable. Change your strategy. Find friends to help. Use will power. Don't let go of your goals. Don't wallow in self pity. You will learn from this difficult time as you let go of the past and move towards the future.

> Allow your intuition to guide you. It is just when you stop trying to make things happen that they do.

Phase 6

> Working on removing the obstruction pays off. Just when you feel this problem will never go away and are about to give up, the power of your determination attracts new help and the obstruction is overcome.

Phase 5

> Stop. Be open to a new way. Seek help from outside.

Phase 4

> You can't force movement. Wait while relying on your own strength.

Phase 3

> When the obstruction is not caused by you it is a matter of fate. Face it without flinching. Take one step at a time.

Phase 2

> You feel frustrated. Stop and make a new plan. It won't happen immediately. Be observant. Don't waste energy on blame of any kind. After dealing with this obstruction you will be stronger.

Phase 1

The Six Phases ↑ of *Obstruction/Limping*

Prescription for *40. Deliverance/Release*

Water then Thunder

 Hsieh

Clear up lingering issues so that you begin with a fresh start. It feels good when any kind of tension has been released. Do not dwell on transgressions made against you. Pardon and forgive. Get on with the new. Solve problems that have held you back in struggle and you will have more energy. You may wake up from something that you have been in denial about. Be like the rain pouring down washing things away as the seeds of the new begin to germinate.

Be clear. Remove all causes with vehemence that created the initial problem. Protect yourself from a set back.

Phase 6

Stay mindful and firm in the decision to be free from the issues or people that caused difficulties.

Phase 5

Detach yourself from those who want something from you that you can't deliver. Be free from people you are not truly connected to so you will attract those who belong with you.

Phase 4

Don't pretend to have more than you do have, thereby inviting people to take it away from you.

Phase 3

Work diligently to be free from the tensions that caused the problem.

Phase 2

After a fight, or release from any difficult time, be still. Enjoy rest and peace.

Phase 1

The Six Phases of *Deliverance/Release*

Prescription for *41. Decrease*

Lake then **Mountain**

 Sun

The sacrifice of decrease cultivates character. Use the power of detachment. This takes effort yet makes way for a new virtue. When you are limited outwardly you can bring focus to your inner world. You may become more intuitive or even psychic in the process. Allow it to happen. If you have negative emotions, work on letting them go. In the restraint needed for letting go there is a different kind of gain oin simplicity. Inner attitude compensates for lacks in the material world.

> Your new lease on life brings good things and blessings to the world. You have helped in giving to the benefit of society in general.

Phase 6

> You are blessed by fate. Nothing can stop you with your plans. You will be showered with riches of the spirit and more than you can now imagine.

Phase 5

> Have no doubts about your new way of relinquishing some physical pleasures. People are attracted to those who work to be free of their own faults.

Phase 4

> If you are alone, you are available for someone to join you. If you are a three some, someone will be unhappy and leave.

Phase 3

> Give and receive. Serve others without diminishing your self. In the process do not try to change anyone.

Phase 2

> You may leave now. Be careful that you bring no harm to those left behind. Help those in need. Be aware of other's feelings in their time of decrease. Be open to the unknown.

Phase 1

The Six Phases ↑ of *Decrease*

Prescription for *42. Increase*

Thunder then **Wind/Wood**

Imitate the good in others while eliminating the bad in yourself. This is the way to increase and self-improvement. When things are working in your favor make use of this time while it lasts. Have a party. Share food in celebration. While you are over flowing with good fortune start a new creative project.

If in your times of increase you can't find it in your heart to help those not as fortunate you will lose what you have gained.

Phase 6

Kindness does not expect praise but receives in the giving.

Phase 5

Do not be selfish with your good fortune. Spread your wealth. When you are generous to others you are being generous to yourself as well.

Phase 4

When blessed with good fortune you exude vibrations that bring strength to those who are not as fortunate as you. When you experience what seems like a bad event expect a blessing in disguise to come from it.

Phase 3

Strive to unite your conscious and unconscious mind with spirit. When you have created a bountiful situation good fortune is yours without fail. When you are in tune with what is right you can help the world beyond yourself.

Phase 2

When you have good luck make sure that you use it with responsibility. Find a way to express your good fortune.

Phase 1

The Six Phases of *Increase*

Prescription for *43. Break-through*  *Kuai*

Heaven then **Lake**

Respond quickly to what is calling you now. Declare your decision. Let go of the past. Focus. Direct your plan into action. Move quickly. Trust your instincts. Be clear about where you are going. Have confidence and confront all obstacles to your chosen path. Don't listen to negativity whether coming from without or within. Any problems you face will make you stronger. Make your dream real.

If you don't do it now you never will and live to regret it.

Phase 6

Big changes will come with your break through. Go for it without hesitation.

Phase 5

Do not let other's negativity influence you. Be strong in yourself. If you feel alone now trust your decision. Do not impose your ideas on people who don't want them.

Phase 4

If you encounter people who do not agree with your plan and try to talk you out of it ignore them and do not tell them what you are doing. Stay true to your self even if you have to go it alone.

Phase 3

Be prepared. You may feel tense and afraid that you are not up to the task. Let go of any fears from the past. by facing them.

Phase 2

In the beginning be most careful. Do only what you are ready to do now.

Phase 1

The Six Phases ↑ of *Break-through*

Prescription for *44. Coming to Meet/Coupling*

Wind/Wood then **Heaven**

 *Kou*

You may have an unexpected predestined encounter. Welcome what comes your way. Magnetism and primal forces are at work. Feminine energy comes to meet the masculine. This contact will be powerful and passionate but may not last. She is a queen with strong feminine power that cannot be controlled. Sex does not always lead to marriage. Enjoy this wonderful time.

Don't over indulge. If the relationship has been all about sex you may be confused about how to handle this for a while.

Phase 6

This is a new time that brings new life and inspiration. Fate provides the fruits of life to be enjoyed.

Phase 5

If you find this encounter disappointing with nothing in it for you remain friendly and considerate. Keep the friendship that is there.

Phase 4

After being by yourself for a while it is your destiny to find someone new. Remain undecided until your path for action becomes clear. You may want to get some outside advice.

Phase 3

Remain withdrawn for a while longer. Think about it. Keep in control.

Phase 2

At first this encounter may feel like a trap. Don't attempt to control anything now or become entangled with a situation that you can't handle.

Phase 1

The Six Phases ↑ of *Coming to Meet/Coupling*

Prescription for *45. Gathering Together*

Earth then Lake

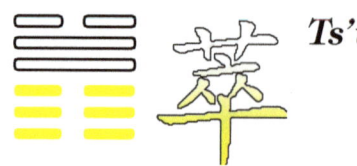 *Ts'ui*

when the entire clan gathers together in community be prepared for unforeseen events. Be on guard. When many people get together in one group there are bound to be some differences among you. A good leader is needed to preside over this event. Is that you? Know the direction you want to take. Find people to help with the project. The way to work together is by being united though a common goal.

> You may be misunderstood about your reasons for joining the group. Work on clearing up these misunderstandings and all will go well.

Phase 6

> If you become the leader of a group there will be people who want to become associated with you, not out of a real connection but for personal gain. Mistrust might happen. Work to create a true bond.

Phase 5

> Work for the good of the group. Take a risk, show what you can do and you will be appreciated.

Phase 4

> When first joining a group you may feel like an outsider and that you won't belong. Align yourself with the leader of the group and you will feel more comfortable.

Phase 3

> When you are led to a group you truly belong with you understand each other immediately. Invite others to join the group.

Phase 2

> At the first gathering there is confusion until people feel comfortable. In a large group one needs a leader to take charge and once one is found the group will coalesce.

Phase 1

The Six Phases ↑ of *Gathering Together*

Prescription for *46. Pushing Upward*  Shên

Wind/Wood then **Earth**

Identify with the power of the time you are living in and ride with that energy. Have a clear goal. Find your hidden potential. Use your will to rise from obscurity to being known in the world. Cultivate people who will help you in your climb to power and recognition. Adapt to what ever is necessary and keep on keeping on with step by step process and you will be successful.

> Always be careful with your choices. If you have blindly followed the path that is not really yours you will wake up to that fact and find yourself tired and will have to begin again.

Phase 6

> You may become drunk with the power of success. Be careful. Proceed slowly and don't leave anything out of your process.

Phase 5

> When you have identified with and matured with the goal of your soul, what you achieve will last beyond your life time. You might even become famous.

Phase 4

> Things open up when you find the right environment. Enjoy being in the right place at the right time.

Phase 3

> You may feel slightly awkward or not up to the task at first. But if you are acting out of your own truth and integrity you will be accepted. Follow your heart for what you really want.

Phase 2

> A new time and adventure begins. Pick a group that you identify with to make your rise to power easier. Communicate clearly. The seeds you plant now are important for success later.

Phase 1

The Six Phases ↑ of *Pushing Upward*

Prescription for *47. Exhaustion/Oppression*   K'un

Water then Lake

Accept the fate that is dealt to you now while remaining true to yourself. What doesn't kill you makes you stronger. Remain cheerful so that you are not overwhelmed by adversity. You feel isolated from those who matter to you. You doubt who your real friends are. Some may give you the wrong advice. Seek help from those you trust. Ignore those who may not believe in you. Nothing you say now will make any difference so lay low. This is a time when you learn what is real and what you can rely on.

> Eventually the oppression or depression will lift. Don't wallow in feeling sorry for yourself by dwelling on what has happened. It is time to move on.

Phase 6

> You may not find help from people around you. Remain quiet and stick to what you know as your truth. Continue with meditation and prayer.

Phase 5

> Help will appear when you are open to it. Trust. You can and will slowly improve the situation.

Phase 4

> When things are going badly you may make fruitless efforts to avoid the pain. Do not depend on things that can't support you. Meditate to help to alleviate depression.

Phase 3

> Outwardly things may appear to be good. While you eat and drink you still feel depressed. Pray even though you don't believe in prayer. Be patient. Help will come.

Phase 2

> Be strong within no matter what cards you have been dealt. Don't allow yourself to become overwhelmed by events. Don't identify with the victim role.

Phase 1

The Six Phases ↑ of *Exhaustion/Oppression*

Prescription for *48. The Well*

Wind/Wood then Water

 *Ching*

It is time to go to the well of the foundation of life, and draw on the inexhaustible spring of the divine in your own nature. Penetrate the deepest part of yourself that gives you life. All humans contain within them the same basic characteristics. Respect others as yourself. You can change where you live but you can't change your real nature that springs from deep within yourself.

> With a spirit that shares with all you become a reliable wellspring of knowledge. You will be nourished and enriched by this inexhaustible well of give and take.

Phase 6

> You can help others by making available what you have learned while delving into the well of your source of inspiration.

Phase 5

> Work on yourself and eventually people will be drawn to you for the qualities you have developed.

Phase 4

> You may be sad for a time when no one notices that you have blessings to share and no one seems to care. Let it be for now. Things will change.

Phase 3

> Find clarity and then cultivate the good in yourself.

Phase 2

> If you wallow in the mud in your life no one will come near you. Think about what you may have to offer.

Phase 1

The Six Phases ↑ of *The Well*

Prescription for *49. Revolution/Molting*

Fire then Lake

 Ko

Times change and so must you. However this personal revolution should be undertaken only when the situation deems it necessary. When you are clear that the time is right then go about these life changing events with care. This is a time of renewal and radical change when you shed your old skin to become new again. Release all past negatives. Trust the process.

> After your revolution of shedding the old and things have settled down there will always be people who will ask, *Why did you do that?* Don't expect everyone to understand or agree with your plans. Be accepting of yourself and your revolution.

Phase 6

> Because the shedding of your past is done with clarity and truth people who may other wise be shocked will understand.

Phase 5

> You will do the right thing when your action for creating a big change of shedding your old ways comes from the true spirit of your unconscious.

Phase 4

> After mulling the situation over for three days or three weeks or three hours, what ever it takes, and you still feel confident in your decision, do not hesitate to take action any longer. Go for it now!

Phase 3

> When you have tried everything and still want a different mode of living you need to prepare. There will be no going back so try to imagine now what this revolution will bring to your life.

Phase 2

> Make the change only when you there is nothing else that can be done. Wait a while before acting. Meditate on your plan.

Phase 1

 76

The Six Phases ↑ of *Revolution/Molting*

Prescription for *50. The Caldron/Transformation*  *Ting*

Wind/Wood then **Fire**

The Caldron is a vessel that is used for transformation of food and also a symbol for the act of transforming the mind and spirit. Burn through the old dead wood of your life and use the flames of your imagination. Let your creative ideas "cook," transforming them into food for thought or food to eat for yourself as well as for others. Be mindful and take responsibility for what you put in the pot.

Success! When transformation is accomplished you will have earned it.

Phase 6

With the right attitude you can find someone to help you in your task and succeed. Be humble and approachable. Serve the "food" you have prepared. Show your work of art. People will love it.

Phase 5

Sometimes you would like to achieve something truly transformational and you are not up to the task. Perhaps you did not work hard enough or you wasted your time with the wrong people. Face reality.

Phase 4

After you accomplished something of worth you may not be recognized. You wrote your great book, painted a master piece, or even cooked a fabulous meal, and no one noticed. If your work is really good in time it will be recognized. This is all part of the process of transformation.

Phase 3

Your achievements may be envied by others. Don't pay attention to negativity that may come from within your self or from others.

Phase 2

Remove from your life all that is stagnant. Turn things upside down to get a fresh start.

Phase 1

The Six Phases of *The Caldron/Transformation*

Prescription for *51. Shock*

Thunder   then   Thunder  Chên

Some times we experience a sudden terrifying shock of fate that feels like an earthquake. There may be many shocks one after another. Remain calm no matter what is happening in these events when you have no control. Examine your heart. Be grateful for what you have and celebrate life while you have it. You may be inspired to do something you never thought of until now. Maybe do something that will make you laugh. Stay focused no matter what distractions come your way.

> The shock of fate, like an earthquake or hurricane, will cause you to lose balance for a while. This is a time when it is especially important to remain composed and not be affected inwardly. This is hard to do but necessary for your wellbeing.

Phase 6

> If you experience many shocks, one after the other, the only thing you can do is focus and stay centered. When the shock passes you will return to normal.

Phase 5

> Do not get stuck in fear, the mire of your mind.

Phase 4

> There are three kinds of shock: Shock like thunder, a shock of fate and shock of the heart. When you experience the shock of fate you may become rattled and not think clearly. Be mindful and maintain your inner composure.

Phase 3

> During the time of shock you may lose things that are precious to you. Don't worry or try to do anything about that now. After the shock is over things will return to normal.

Phase 2

> At the burst of the shock you are shaken to your core and you may feel weak and scared. You will be fine. You may even laugh when the ordeal is over.

Phase 1

The Six Phases ↑ of *Shock*

Prescription for *52. Keeping Still/Meditation*

Mountain then Mountain  Kên

This is a time for inner work. Quieting the heart is difficult. It is important to know when it is a time for rest and meditation or when it is the time for movement. Meditation is the end and the beginning of a process. If you become quiet and drop the ego for a while you can see what is happening in a clearer way. You can see where you belongs in the scheme of things. Be like a mountain, keeping still. *"Be here now."*

After practicing mindfulness meditation one accepts what is in the state of peace.

Phase 6

It is wise to always be mindful of what you talk about.

Phase 5

Keep working on leaving your ego out of the situation. This will help you on the path to mindful awareness.

Phase 4

Don't force the process of quieting your mind. That can have the opposite effect of causing unnecessary stress.

Phase 3

You can't save or change anyone but yourself.

Phase 2

Be here now.

Phase 1

The Six Phases ↑ of *Keeping Still/Meditation*

Prescription for *53. Gradual Progress*

Mountain then Wind/Wood

 *Chien*

Take your time to insure the right action. Proceed slowly step by step in tranquility. Don't try to convince others of your way of doing things. Develop influence by your actions and good character. Be persistent, gentle and adaptable.

At the end of your life, after a long road of living the path of continual gradual progress you will become a shining example for others to emulate.

Phase 6

In your slow gradual development you might feel that you are making no progress at all and wonder what you are doing. Trust in yourself. You will get there.

Phase 5

In the middle of the struggle to develop, relax, rest and absorb what you have developed so far.

Phase 4

When you proceed too quickly you might make a mistake that you cannot foresee and your development may feel like it is taking a step backwards. Meditate on right action now.

Phase 3

Share what you have and what you have learned on your path of development.

Phase 2

Begin very slowly. Do not look for outside help now. Develop your own path and way of doing things.

Phase 1

The Six Phases ↑ of *Gradual Progress*

Prescription for 54. The Second Wife   *Kuei Mei*

Lake then **Thunder**

When you are the second wife you must be careful. You are not here to replace the first wife. Your relationship is based on love and attraction so it does not matter about the rest of society's conventions. You will be protected. Be mindful of why you are here and what you want. All relationships have difficulties to over come. You may find yourself in a situation that needs a change. Accept that fate is at work here.

> If the arrangement you are involved in doesn't work out you can always leave. This is your choice.

Phase 6

> If you have had to wait a long time to find a mate you may have to accept the limitations of what is available.

Phase 5

> If you do not want to take this offer now you can wait for another opportunity.

Phase 4

> Yes, it is difficult to hold a positive self image in this situation. In the long run you will be recognized for your fine qualities.

Phase 3

> You may feel disappointed playing second fiddle. Stick it out for a while and see what happens. Be observant and learn.

Phase 2

> You may lack personal power when entering a relationship with a person who had a deep past of experience before you ever appeared. Be aware of all that has been before you without judging it or feeling inadequate. You are there for a reason.

Phase 1

The Six Phases ↑ of *The Second Wife*

Prescription for 55. Abundance

Fire   then   Thunder

 Fêng

Abundance is like the fullness of summer time with plenty for the harvest. If you have achieved some things that you have wanted to experience be grateful for that and don't worry about what you could not do. No one can do everything. Enjoy to the fullest what you have now. Be generous. Nothing lasts forever.

> Once you achieve abundance of recognition, don't be arrogant about it. Do not forget the friends and family who have supported you or you may lose all that you have gained.

Phase 6

> You are able to attract people like yourself who will help you in ways you don't yet imagine. Be ready for many blessings to come your way.

Phase 5

> You attract those of like mind by combining energy with wisdom of what you have learned.

Phase 4

> Sometimes you may feel invisible. It happens to all of us sooner or later in one way or another. This is just life as it plays out. Accept that there is nothing you can do about that fact.

Phase 3

> When things happen that cloud the reality of a situation, stay mindful of the truth as you know it. Your force of character will influence the situation in the right direction.

Phase 2

> When you find someone that you know is like you and are meant to spend time with, go for it wholeheartedly.

Phase 1

The Six Phases ↑ of *Abundance*

Prescription for *56. The Wanderer*

Mountain then **Fire**

Lü

When traveling in places where you don't know the customs or the people it is important to leave all self-importance at home. Be adaptable to the new or strange surroundings. Choose your traveling companions carefully. While traveling you will meet many people and have relationships that are not long lasting. Always be a good guest.

> When traveling you must always be conscious of being a stranger in a strange land or you could lose your welcome there.

Phase 6

> After a while you will find friends and may decide to stay in your new place of travel.

Phase 5

> Find a place to stay. You may even decide to live in this new place for a while. Don't be surprised if at times you feel homesick.

Phase 4

> In a strange land with strange people it is important to know what the rules are and abide by them or you may find yourself in the kind of trouble that you can't get out of.

Phase 3

> Find a friend or companion to travel with who can be helpful on your journey to new places.

Phase 2

> While traveling remain open, humble and respectful of your new and foreign surroundings.

Phase 1

The Six Phases ↑ of *The Wanderer*

Prescription for *57. Gentle Penetration*

Wind/Wood then **Wind/Wood**

The Gentle Wind and Wood is about having gradual and inconspicuous influence that never ceases. To act in this way may not cause a sensation right away but the effects will last. Have a goal and stick with it. Be like the wind, invisible in itself, permeating, penetrating and powerful in its effect.

Don't spend your energy now dwelling on the mysteries of past mistakes or try to penetrate into the unknown arenas that you cannot do anything about.

Phase 6

Make up your mind what to do and then **DO** it!

Phase 5

Slowly, through experience, you achieve the success you hoped for.

Phase 4

The time has arrived for you to take a new direction. Think over your plan of action carefully. Note where you have been, where you are and where you might be going.

Phase 3

Hidden obstacles, like ghosts that you can't see or touch, are in your way. Bring to consciousness what is preventing you from progress now. See a therapist, a doctor, an astrologer or get an I Ching reading about the situation to gain understanding and become free from the block.

Phase 2

Have no doubt about your goal. Be decisive in action. Don't be wishy-washy in your effort to penetrate the situation.

Phase 1

The Six Phases ↑ of *Gentle Penetration*

Prescription for *58. Joy*

Lake) then Lake) 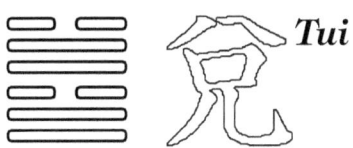 Tui

When you feel and express joy you affect those around you and people will want to be in your presence. You learn by talking with friends and sharing in the discussion. There is double joy when people interact and replenish each other. Perhaps give a party to celebrate and share the joy with others.

When you are continually seduced by outward pleasures you take your chances. So be it!

Phase 6

From time to time we all have temptations. Before indulging ask yourself what the price may be. Protect yourself with awareness of the outcome.

Phase 5

Do you find joy in passion of the body or pleasures of the mind? Your choice.

Phase 4

Real joy must be experienced within yourself. You should not look for distractions from your true nature to substitute for pleasure. This can lead to addiction.

Phase 3

Find joy and pleasure in ways that do not harm your health.

Phase 2

It is wonderful when you can feel joy that is not dependent on anything outside of your self.

Phase 1

The Six Phases ↑ of *Joy*

Prescription for *59. Dispersion*

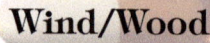 then

Huan

Let the ice melt that is frozen in your veins from previous hurts. Dispel illusions and misunderstandings. Remove obstacles that were created in the past so that you can have what is coming in the future. If you can keep your ego in check this will help to gather around you kindred souls. Have a "Thanksgiving." Celebrate what you all share with music and food.

Keep your family away from any trouble that the group may cause. If something is harmful to your family you may have to leave. Only you will know what is the right action to take.

Phase 6

Group activity can have a goal that reaches far beyond that of any one person within the group. Personal misunderstandings must be dealt with and eliminated for the sake of the common goal.

Phase 5

When you are working for the good of the group you must have a broad view of where you are all headed.

Phase 4

When things seem too difficult, try to park your ego and let a larger view of life carry you through.

Phase 3

Align yourself with people who support you. If you find yourself in a bad mood do not dump your feelings on others. Your goal is to attract what you like, not the negativity you may hide in yourself.

Phase 2

If you have discord or misunderstandings with anyone in the group, clear those things up right away before they grow into something too big to deal with.

Phase 1

The Six Phases ↑ of *Dispersion*

Prescription for *60. Limitation*

Lake then *Water*

It is necessary to have limits in life. Everything has a limit and a measurement. The hours in a day, days in a year, years in a century, the solar system in the galaxy are all within a limitation of measurement. It is also just as important not to be extreme by limiting yourself with unnecessary restrictions. Make things clear by defining what your limitations are and then set your limits in order to have balance in your life.

Remember not to impose limitations that are too strict for yourself or others.

Phase 6

Applying a limitation effectively can have its own rewards. For example, limiting food intake can be beneficial at times. Do not expect to impose limitations on others that you yourself will not carry out.

Phase 5

Some limitations originate in nature and can be helpful when you use them to your advantage.

Phase 4

Be aware of your own limits and work within those parameters. If you misjudge these limitations don't blame anyone else on what happens.

Phase 3

There is a time for action. Don't miss an opportunity. Don't limit yourself when you don't need to.

Phase 2

Find out what your limitations are before beginning any task. There are limits within yourself and limits imposed from outside.

Phase 1

The Six Phases of Limitation

Prescription for *61. Inner Truth*

Lake then Wind/Wood

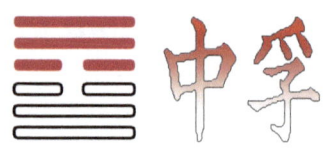 *Chung Fu*

When you act from inner truth you are able to influence difficult people by learning who they are and what motivates them. Keep an open mind and open heart, free of preconceptions. Make an effort to connect. Be sympathetic. Maintain mutual interest. When others see that you understand them they will be open to you in return. Align your fantasies and dreams with outer reality to maintain inner truth within yourself.

Inner truth is not based on what others say, but what you know and who you are inside.

Phase 6

The power of being centered emanates outward. You influence and help others with strength of character.

Phase 5

For your own peace of mind maintain humility by not caring about what others are thinking or doing. Always follow your own path.

Phase 4

You find friends. But no matter how well you get along, it is important to maintain your feeling of well being without depending on being liked or appreciated.

Phase 3

True spiritual or heartfelt affinity is an energy that emanates from you without conscious effort and is felt by those of kindred soul and spirit. This is not an effect you can create with your will. Inner truth works from the center of the heart, soul-to-soul.

Phase 2

Begin by being prepared with your own inner stability. This means having no secret relationships that you cannot rely on. Don't take on someone else's problems.

Phase 1

 88

The Six Phases ↑ of *Inner Truth*

Prescription for *62. Many Small Things*   *Hsiao Kuo*

Mountain then **Thunder**

You cannot always do what you would like to do. At such times you must accept what you can do. Work with and pay attention to the details.

When the task is difficult and you try to go beyond your limits you invite disaster.

Phase 6

You can do something more important and take on a larger task when you get help from people who have the kind of skills that you need for the job.

Phase 5

Don't force any situation. Be on guard and use extreme caution.

Phase 4

Don't take on more than you can do now. Be careful. Pay attention to the little things to avoid big mistakes.

Phase 3

You find yourself in an exceptional situation. Ask the female members of your family for guidance. Rely on your own yin energy.

Phase 2

Accept the fact when you don't always have the strength to tackle a job beyond your capabilities. Just knowing this will save a lot of wasted energy.

Phase 1

The Six Phases of *Many Small Things*

Prescription for 63. After Completion   既濟 Chi Chi

Fire then **Water**

You have completed your task, everything is in order and you are celebrating. Caution! Keep in mind that when things are in perfect order this is the time when everything can change again and return to disorder. You should prevent hubris that could cause things to fall apart too soon.

After completing the big project, if you think about what you could have done or should have done, you will ruin your sense of achievement and you won't change a thing. Don't look back. Be still.

Phase 6

Be thankful for your blessings and grateful for all that you have accomplished.

Phase 5

Remain extra cautious now. You don't know what you don't know.

Phase 4

When everything is completed for this task lay low for a while and see what unfolds in the new situation of completion.

Phase 3

Don't expect special recognition now just because you have completed something big or important. Recognition will inevitably come to you but do not run after it. What truly belongs to you cannot be taken away.

Phase 2

Completion! You are drunk with happiness. Stop for a while and reflect so that you are not knocked down by the unexpected.

Phase 1

The Six Phases ↑ of *After Completion*

Prescription for *64. Before Completion*

Water then **Fire**

This is the moment just before you bring something to conclusion. This is the place of potential. Everything is in proper order for a major transition. Even so, be wary. Don't be smug or relax too much. Be on the lookout for unexpected events coming from outside that could prevent you from completing this task.

Bring out the champagne and truly celebrate the beginning of a new era. Just try not to get drunk.
At every ending there is a new beginning.

Phase 6

Yea! You did it! You move into a new era and it is time for celebration of completion of the old way.

Phase 5

Don't doubt yourself now. You are in transition which is always a struggle. You are preparing for a new kind of future.

Phase 4

You may feel too weak to continue. Don't give up. Get help. You don't have to do everything alone.

Phase 3

Moving slowly now is not the same as being lazy. Keep your eyes on the goal and you will get there when the time is right.

Phase 2

Don't be tempted to rush through the tasks necessary to complete your project. Hurrying can cause unforeseen delays.

Phase 1

The Six Phases ↑ of *Before Completion*

Hexagram 10 — Treading

The Image of Heaven over Lake

Adele

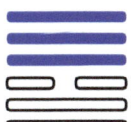 # HEXAGRAM 10 — TREADING

The Image of Heaven over Lake

My contained power of restraint is released and I tread
Into manner and mode of expression.
Using a creative spirit with joy and humor I develop personality.
I accept my varying and unequal character traits
By giving them expression in appropriate ways.
Moving with strength, while treading carefully
I handle unknown dangers by
Allowing my thinking to be led by deeper intuitions.
I protect myself while pleasing others as I
Walk with the mask of a tiger.

Nine in the First Place

Tiger like I move surely on the path ... alone.

Nine in the Second Place

Looking straight ahead I go deeper
Into my dark tiger-self
As my instincts show the way.

Six in the Third Place

I stumble and do not see clearly
When I am swallowed by my persona.
In the weakness of fear
My mask of aggression engulfs me.

Nine in the Fourth Place

I feel the strength of powerful animal instincts
Taking care not to confuse myself with the tiger.

Nine in the Fifth Place

I am aware of my wildness and move with it.

Nine in the Last Place

Success in movement is like a hunt or a dance.
Power is in the process.
Quality of performance is the result of the care
In each step taken.
The tiger, the path and I are one.

Earlier Heaven: Primal Arangment of Trigrams

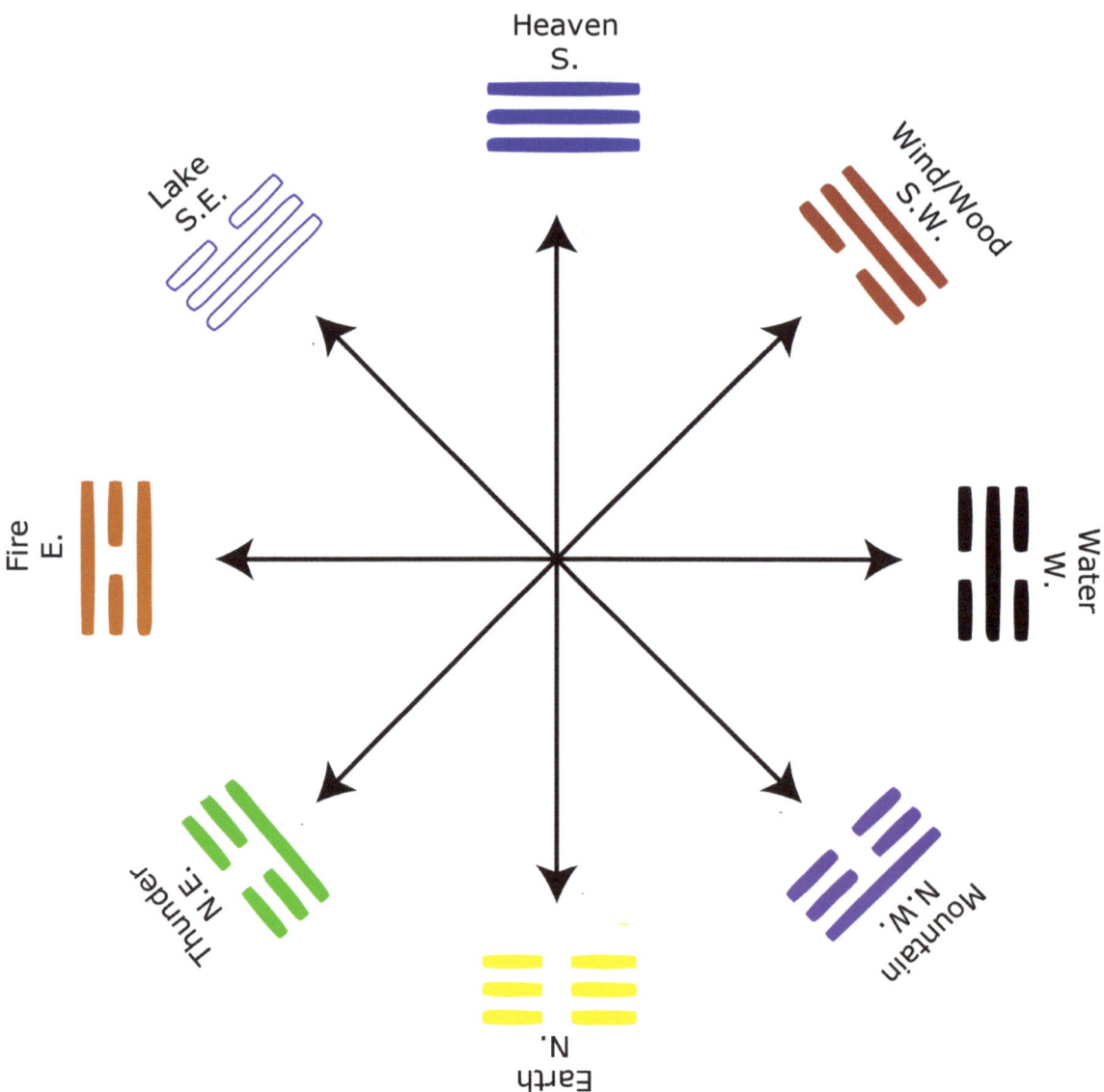

The Primal arrangement, the sequence of Earlier Heaven, represents the world of thoughts, wishes, motives, ideas, unobservable things, way of thinking and the spirit or influence behind all actions. It is arranged in the polarity; the complementary of opposites.

Later Heaven: Inner World Arangment of Trigrams

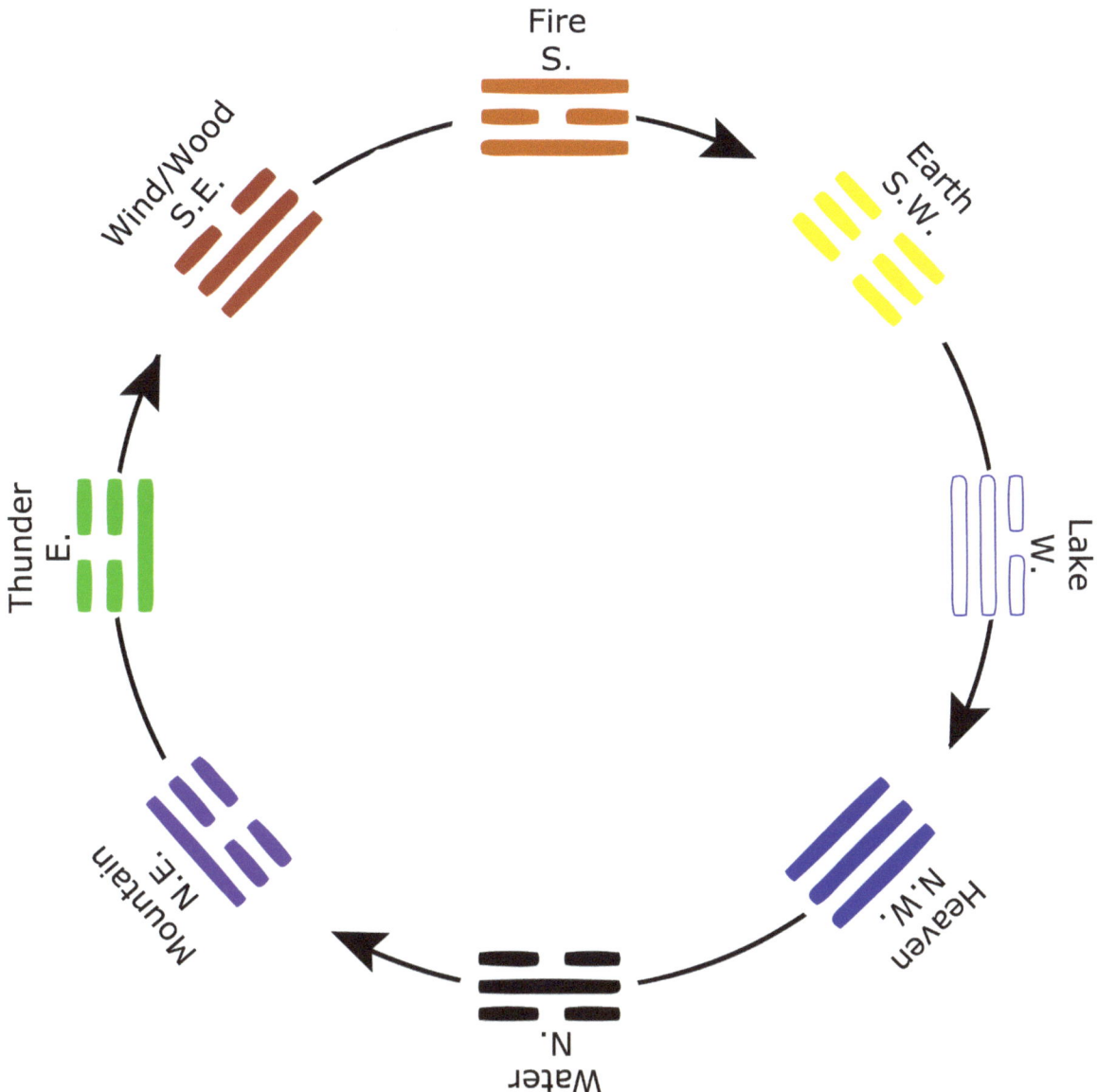

The world of thought shines through this sequence of Later heaven. It represents the world of phenomena and the senses. It is the seasonal cycle of nature, growth and decay, moving clockwise. This represents the cast hexagram in the world of manifestation, phenomena, and observable things.

BIBLIOGRAPHY

Anthony, Carol K. A. *A Guide to the I Ching.* Stow, MA: Anthony Publishing Company 1980.

Cleary, Thomas (Translator) Lui I-Ming (Author). *The Taoist I Ching.* Boston, MA: Shambhala Publications,1986.

Cleary, Thomas, *I Ching Mandalas: A Program of Study for The Book of Changes.* Boston, MA: Shambhala Publications 1989.

Hook, Diana Ffarington, *The I Ching and Mankind.* London and Boston: Routledge & Kegan Paul Ltd 1975.

Hook, Diana Ffarington, *The I Ching and You.* New York, NY: E. P. Dutton 1973.

Karcher, Stephen. *Total I Ching: Myths for Change.* London, England: Little, Brown Group 2008.

Ritsema, Rudolf and Stephen Karcher. *I Ching: The Classic Chinese Oracle of Change: The First Complete Translation With Concordance.* New York, NY: Barns & Noble, Inc., Element Books 1995.

Sloane, Sarah Jane, T*he I Ching for Writers: Finding the Page Inside You.* Novato, CA: New World Library 2005.

Wilhelm, Helmut (Author) Cary F. Baynes (Translator). *Changes: Eight lectures on the I Ching.* New York, NY: Bollingen Foundation by Pantheon Books. Inc. 1960.

Wilhelm, Richard, Cary F. Baynes, Hellmut Wilhelm and C. G. Jung. *The I Ching or Book of Changes,* Bollingen Foundation, New York, NY: by Princeton University Press, Princeton, NJ 1967.

Afterword

As I was completing this book I had an experience with the I Ching I will share with the reader. After the graphics were tweaked and changed, I had to add a few pages. There was nothing involved that should have taken me very long to do. Suddenly, BAM! I couldn't go on with the process. I could do anything else but finish this book. The feeling was something akin to having invisible, and yet very strong chains around me. I was desperate. I wished that I could talk to a therapist about my problem; not any therapist — one familiar with the I Ching. That wasn't going to happen. So, as is my habit, I decided to consult the I Ching about my block to completing this book, asking Carl Jung to speak to me through the I Ching since I could not speak to him directly. My logic in such imaginative questions is that it doesn't cost me anything, and maybe it will help me with my issue of being unable to proceed with finishing my book.

I threw the coins and got hexagram number 64, *Before Completion*. As usual, the I Ching reflected back to me exactly where I was — in the stage of just before completion of my book. But what rocked my mind was that all six lines were changing, and when all lines in the hexagram *Before Completion* change, the hexagram turns into number 63, *After Completion*. Perfect! I was stunned! For one thing, having all six lines change is a very very rare event. I contacted Luis Andrade, an I Chinger I know of from the Internet. I figured he knows a lot about the I Ching in several languages and hoped he could tell me what the odds are for having all six lines change. Luis sent me a chart of the statistics of the varying odds of getting combinations of changing lines. If you have 3 yang lines and 3 yin lines that change to their opposites, the odds are 1 in 13,107 that you will receive this configuration.

There were a number of awesome aspects to this reading:

- That I got all changing lines, a chance of 1 in 13,107.
- The I Ching responded exactly to the dilemma I was asking about. It always does, but sometimes the response is not so obvious.
- The fact that I received all changing lines had yet another significance. The intent of this book, already discussed in the Introduction, is about treating the I Ching "as if" one got all moving lines when seeking guidance for a situation. The I Ching threw me back to myself.

When I settled down from my excitement and read what I had written for *Before Completion* in these *Prescriptions,* the advice seemed so obvious. I then thought, *Why am I not taking the advice I am giving here in this book? Why did I not prescribe for myself what the I Ching says in the situation of Before Completion?*

When I read my own prescription for

Before Completion, there it was: explaining, and advising just what I was working on. I skipped over the top paragraph for the general meaning of the hexagram add focused on what I had written for line 2,

"Moving slowly now is not the same as being lazy. Keep your eyes on the goal and you will get there when the time is right."

And in line 4,

"Don't doubt yourself now. You are in transition which is always a struggle. You are preparing for a new kind of future."

If you have never consulted the I Ching by trusting the chance synchronicity of casting the coins you might think, *"Well, so what?"* about getting all changing lines.

If you are a person who is familiar with the I Ching you will appreciate my awe at this reading. You might wonder, how did this reading, so accurate and a chance of 1 in 13,107 effect me? Did I immediately get back to work? Was the block instantly removed? No, it was not. But if you are reading this, obviously I completed the book. What happened at this point was that my angst dropped away. I felt that I'm doing what I am supposed to be doing. The I Ching speaks to me so directly. I feel fortunate to be on this path that is full of rewards, with a heritage of nothing comparable. It's interesting. It's fun. It works.

Obviously, I still consult the I Ching's wisdom by using the coins. But my lesson here was to take my own medicine and use my *I Ching Prescriptions* when I feel the need.

I finished writing this first part of this *Afterword.* I needed a fresh eye and sent my manuscript to Dr. Katya Walter to see if she saw any errors or suggestions for improvement. Katya responded, catching some typos and said she felt I needed to elaborate more about my process when getting this hexagram with the six moving lines in *Before Completion*. I made all the corrections she suggested except for that last one.

I became blocked again. I should have read more carefully what I had written for the general meaning of *Before Completion.*

"This is the moment just before you bring something to conclusion. This is the place of potential. Everything is in proper order for a major transition. Even so, be wary. Don't be smug or relax too much. Be on the lookout for unexpected events coming from outside that could prevent you from completing this task".

On the morning of March 27, 2011 I signed on to the Internet to do my usual reading of various sites, one of them being Rob and Trish MacGregor's blog on synchronicity (http://www.synchrosecrets.com/synchrosecrets/) where they have at times posted some of my own synchronistic experiences. The posting for the day was about the significance of the number 23. In the I Ching, number 23 is the hexagram called *Splitting Apart.* The article mentioned that Elizabeth Taylor had died on the 23rd and then this one simple sentence:

"Jose Arguelles died. He was a visionary of the New Age movement."

I was stunned. Shocked. Saddened beyond words.

I first met José Argüelles in New York in February of 1973, shortly after he and his wife, Miriam wrote their book, **Mandala.** I again met José as my Core faculty from 1978 - 1981 while working on my Ph.D. at the The Union Institute University. My thesis was named *Art and The Personal Symbolic Process.* It included some of my earlier I Ching work. After graduating I created my limited edition version of that work. José wrote a Foreword for it.

There is no one I felt more spiritually connected to than José and as of this writing, have not yet absorbed this news as a full reality. Reading of his death certainly was that unexpected event coming from outside and again delayed completing the last section of this book.

There is more to the story of my I Ching reading, *Before Completion.* On March 19th I dreamed that José came to visit me. Although I had not seen him for 25 years, in the dream he looked the same. He was cheerful and said to me, *"Adele, bring out the champagne. Let's celebrate together."*

Like most dreams, that one was a mystery. What was José wanting to celebrate? I have been studying my dreams long enough to know that even if I didn't understand it, the dream had meaning that would eventually reveal itself.

Four days later José died. When I heard of his death, the dream of his visit came back to my mind and it felt even more mysterious. I experienced the dream as a real visit, so I took the point of view that perhaps that was his way of saying good by and that he did not view death as sad, but as a celebration. Was that a rationalization? Perhaps. I spent the rest of that day doing nothing except for a taking a meditative walk in the woods. Then I looked again at what I had written in the sixth phase of *Before Completion:*

"Bring out the champagne and truly celebrate the beginning of a new era. Just try not to get drunk.

At every ending there is a new beginning."

As of this date, my interpretation of the dream is that Jose did in fact visit me in my dream. I am not advanced enough in my spiritual development to celebrate the death of anyone, especially someone I love. But had I not had the dream, had I not gotten stuck completing this piece of writing, had Katya not said to tell more about this process, I would not be writing so intimately about José Argüelles. I know he would celebrate with me the *Before Completion* turning into *After Completion a*nd here he is brought to our awareness in these pages.

Adele Aldridge, March 31, 2011

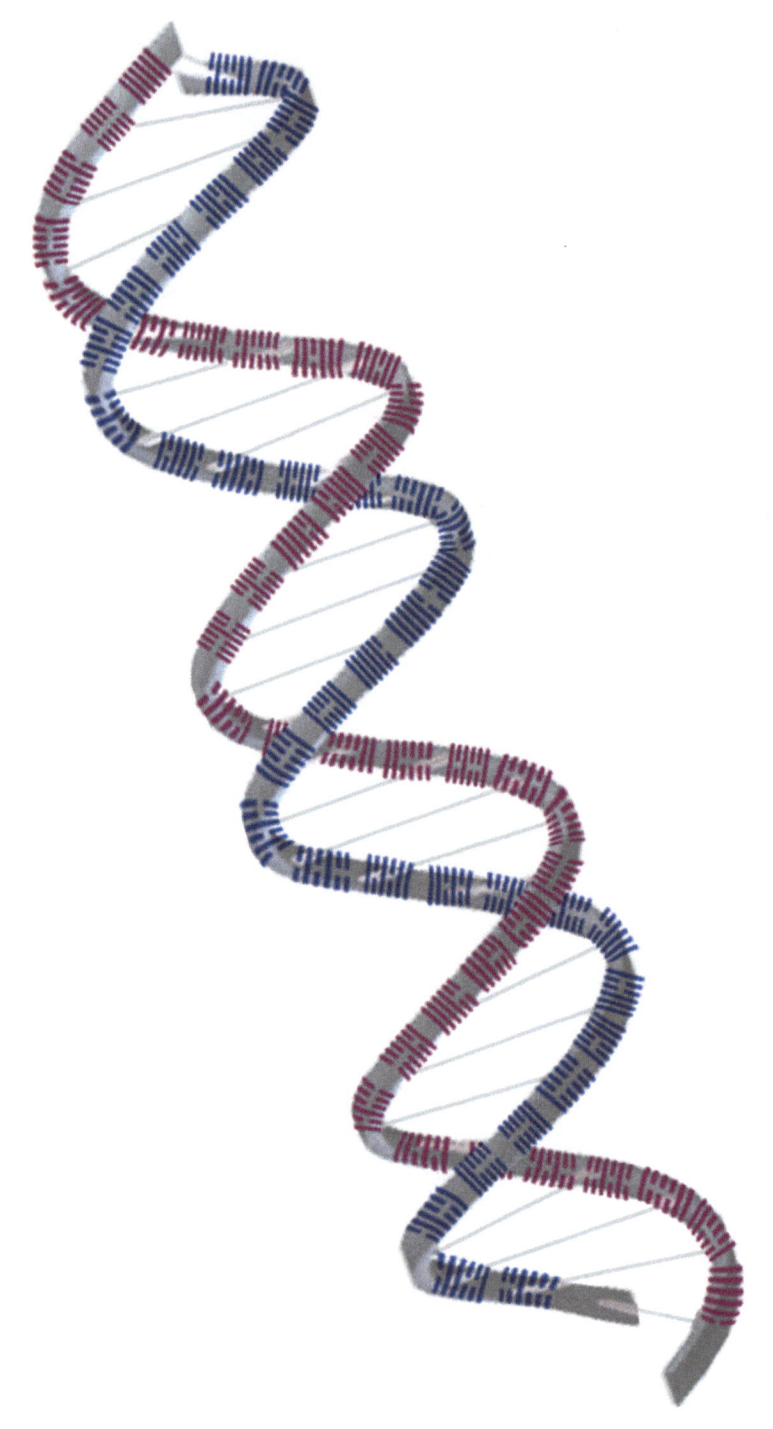

ABOUT THE AUTHOR

Adele Aldridge has been working with the I Ching for 40 years as a learner and as an artist creating images and text for *I Ching Meditations — A Woman's Book of Changes.* She earned a Ph.D. in Art and the Personal Symbolic Process, studying with José Argüelles at the Union Institute University. She has thirty-five years of experience as a fine artist showing her work in galleries in New York, Connecticut and San Francisco, and has worked as a Book Illustrator, Graphic Designer, Web Designer and Instructor in Computer Graphic programs. You can learn more about Adele Aldridge's work with the I Ching at: www.ichingmeditations.com.

ABOUT KATYA WALTER

Katya Walter has an interdisciplinary Ph.D. She spent 5 years of post-doctoral study at the Jung Institute of Zurich, and a year of post-study in China. Dr. Walter taught in colleges and universities in the USA and abroad for sixteen years before focusing on writing, lecturing, and workshops. Dr. Walter is author of the *Touching God's TOE* series of books.: Vol. 1: *Tao of Chaos: Merging East and West.* Vol. 2: *Double Bubble Universe,* Vol. 3: *The Universe is Alive & Well,* Vol. 4: *The Universal Fractal Tree,* Vol. 5: *Fractal Gravitons,* Vol. 6: *Quantum Organics.* She also authored *Dream Mail,* a handbook on the fractal messages carried in the deeper structure of dreams. Her web site is http://doublebubbleuniverse.com

ABOUT REBECCA REDFIELD

Rebecca Redfield has been a life-long student of the I Ching. In pursuit of a major in Linguistics, she studied 5 foreign languages at the University of Wisconsin, Madison. Rebecca naturally looks for the message expressed in the language of clouds, the cries of birds or a gust of wind. She's recently written a book about the way the trigrams speak to her, called *Eight Trigrams for Serenity and Mindfulness.*